Mission
San Gabriel
Arcángel
(1771)

Pueblo of
Los Angeles

Mission
San Juan
Capistrano
(1776)

Mission
San Luis Rey
de Francia
(1798)

Mission
San Diego
de Alcalá
(1769)

Alta California
Baja California

Mission
San Fernando
Rey de España
(1797)

Presidio
of
San Diego

Mission
Santa Inés
(1804)

Mission
San Buenaventura
(1782)

Presidio of
Santa Bárbara

Mission
Santa
Bárbara
(1786)

Santa
Barbara
Channel

Channel Islands

Mission
La Purísima
Concepción
(1787)

The MISSIONS of CALIFORNIA

The MISSIONS of CALIFORNIA

The MISSIONS of CALIFORNIA

BILL YENNE

THUNDER BAY
P·R·E·S·S
SAN DIEGO, CALIFORNIA

Thunder Bay Press

An imprint of the Advantage Publishers Group
5880 Oberlin Drive, San Diego, CA 92121-4794
www.thunderbaybooks.com

Library of Congress Cataloging-in-Publication Data

Yenne, Bill, 1949-
  The Missions of California / Bill Yenne.
    p. cm.
  Includes index.
  ISBN 1-59223-319-8
  1. Missions--California--El Camino Real--History.
2. Catholic Church--Missions--California--El Camino
Real. 3. El Camino Real (Calif.)--Church history. 4.
Catholic Church--California--El Camino Real–
History--18th century. 5. Catholic Church--California–
El Camino Real--History--19th century. I. Title.
  BV2803.C2Y46 2004
  979.4'02--dc22
                                            2004058031
        Printed in China.
        1 2 3 4 5 08 07 06 05 04

Copyright ©2004 Bill Yenne
Cover and text design © 2004 Bill Yenne

AGS BookWorks
P.O. Box 460313
San Francisco, California 94146
yennemissionbook@netscape.net

All photographs are by and © Bill Yenne,
except those appearing as follows, which are courtesy
of the Library of Congress:
Pages 30, 33, 34, 36, 43 (top right), 43 (bottom right),
51, 59 (right), 66 (bottom), 67, 80, 84 (both), 88,
106 (bottom), 118, 120 (bottom), 123, 124,
126 (both), 127, 128 (both), 143, 148, 159, 174, 177,
180, 182, 183.
The illustration on page 72 is from the
personal collection of the author.

This book is dedicated to the author's
mother, who passed away in Santa Cruz in
1997. I wish that she could have lived to
see this book completed. I believe that she
would have enjoyed it.

The photograph on page 1 is of the facade and
campanario at Mission Santa Inés.

The photograph on page 2 is of the reredos at
Mission San Fernando Rey de España.

The photograph above was taken at
Mission San Luis Rey de Francia.

The photograph on page 7 was taken at the entrance
to the cemetery at Mission
San Carlos Borromeo de Carmelo.

The photograph on page 192 is of the altar at
Mission San Juan Bautista.

Table of Contents

THE MISSIONS OF CALIFORNIA

INTRODUCTION

THE MISSIONS OF CALIFORNIA represented the first major organized effort by Europeans to colonize the West Coast of North America. They were the first permanent European settlements in what is now the state of California, and from these settlements would grow several of today's most important California cities, from San Diego to San Francisco.

For most of the mission period in the state's history, which lasted from 1769 to 1834, the missions were the major centers of European population and culture within the state.

California's first highway grew out of the route first taken by Gaspar de Portolá in the first Spanish exploration of California. Known as El Camino Reál, meaning "King's Road" or "Royal Highway," this road linked the missions, and it soon became a major thoroughfare for commercial traffic. Eventually, as missions were consciously placed a day's ride apart along El Camino Reál, the missions became way stations along the road

and an integral part of California life. The missions marked the origin of many aspects of California culture. The first library in California was at Mission San Carlos Borromeo de Carmelo, and the first vineyards in America's most important wine-producing state were located at the missions.

The twenty-one California missions were seen by the missionaries who established and operated them as a means of bringing Christianity to the indigenous people of the various areas of California, but they were supported by the government of Spain as a means of establishing a political presence here. In 1769, as the effort moved forward to establish these missions, the Spanish had been the dominant political power in most of the Western Hemisphere for nearly three centuries, and they hoped to remain as such.

When Christopher Columbus permanently opened the sea lanes between Europe and the Western Hemisphere in 1492, he was sailing

under a Spanish flag and he claimed his discovery for Spain. Of course, no one then knew the full extent of the Western Hemisphere. Portugal, Spain's chief rival at the time, complained that Spain should not be allowed to claim the entirety of the newly discovered continent. Pope Alexander VI intervened to settle the dispute, establishing a longitudinal dividing line 345 miles west of the Cape Verde Islands, and granting Spain all undiscovered lands to the west, and Portugal everything to the east. This did not end the dispute, so in 1494, the two countries met at the Spanish town of Tordesillas to hammer out an agreement, which was eventually endorsed by the pope. The new map pushed the demarcation line nearly a thousand miles west. Portugal gained substantially, but because the lands across the Atlantic Ocean had yet to be mapped, they did not realize that they got just a part of what is now Brazil, while Spain was granted more than 90 percent of the Western Hemisphere.

THE SPANISH FIND CALIFORNIA

IN 1521, HERNANDO CORTEZ (Hernán Cortés) defeated the Aztec emperor Montezuma and the Spanish established their colony of New Spain (Nueva España) on the mainland of North America. Though the Spanish claimed all of North America, they were slow to explore the vast lands in the north of New Spain. Between 1540 and 1542, Francisco Vásquez de Coronado explored much of what is now Arizona and New Mexico in search of the golden cities of Cibola. He did not find them, and Spain showed little further interest in the area. In the meanwhile, in 1535, Cortez led an expedition to the west coast of what is now Mexico. Here, he surveyed the long inlet known since as the Sea of Cortez. Across the inlet was the long, slender strip of land that would be named California. Beyond California lay the Pacific Ocean.

Initially, it was thought that California was a long offshore island.

A few years later, in 1542, Juan Rodríguez Cabrillo sailed up the west coast of California for several hundred miles without reaching the northern tip of the supposed island, and it would be many years before further explorations determined that the lower part of California was merely a peninsula.

After California was discovered, the Spanish divided it into two parts for administrative purposes. The lower part, which was later determined to be a peninsula, was called Lower California, or Baja California. The upper part of the supposed island, which Cabrillo had surveyed from the Pacific Ocean side, was called Upper California, or Alta California. Because Baja California was closest to New Spain, and thus more easily accessible, it would be explored and settled first, although this would not occur for more than sixty years after Cortez had first laid eyes on it.

THE MISSIONARIES ARRIVE

SEBASTIÁN VIZCAÍNO ARRIVED IN Baja California in 1596 to establish the first Spanish colony there. As was to be the case with most Spanish expeditions into territory previously unexplored by Europeans, Catholic priests accompanied the Vizcaíno expedition. Just as Father Marcos de Niza had traveled north at Coronado's side in 1540, Vizcaíno was accompanied by Father Diego de Perdomo,

THE MISSIONS OF CALIFORNIA
(ESTABLISHED BETWEEN 1769 AND 1823)

Mission San Diego de Alcalá (1769)
Mission San Carlos Borromeo de Carmelo (1770)
Mission San Antonio de Padua (1771)
Mission San Gabriel Arcángel (1771)
Mission San Luis Obispo de Tolosa (1772)
Mission San Francisco de Asís (1776)
Mission San Juan Capistrano (1776)
Mission Santa Clara de Asís (1777)
Mission San Buenaventura (1782)
Mission Santa Bárbara (1786)
Mission La Purísima Concepción (1787)
Mission Santa Cruz (1791)
Mission Nuestra Señora de la Soledad (1791)
Mission San José (1797)
Mission San Juan Bautista (1797)
Mission San Miguel Arcángel (1797)
Mission San Fernando Rey de España (1797)
Mission San Luis Rey de Francia (1798)
Mission Santa Inés (1804)
Mission San Rafael Arcángel (1817)
Mission San Francisco de Solano (1823)

Father Bernardino de Zamudio, Father Antonio Tello, and others. They established a small encampment, which they called La Paz.

Because of the harsh and desolate conditions in the deserts of Baja California, this initial settlement effort at La Paz would fail. The missionaries returned to the mainland, and in 1602, Vizcaíno went on to be the first Spanish mariner to conduct a detailed survey of Alta California's coast since Cabrillo sixty years earlier.

In 1683, nearly a century after Vizcaíno's failed venture, Admiral Isidro Antondo y Antillon returned to La Paz to try again to create a permanent settlement in Baja California. With him were a Jesuit priest named Father Pedro Matias Goni, as well as Father José Guijosa, of the Order of St. John of God. Also with them was the Italian-born royal cartographer of California, Eusebio Francisco Kino, who was to become a Jesuit priest the following year. They established

Mission San Bruno, which was the first mission in California, although it would be abandoned in 1685 when the La Paz settlement was abandoned again. In 1684, meanwhile, in his role as a cartographer, Father Kino would be the first Spaniard to cross Baja California by land. He is also credited with later figuring out that Baja California was a peninsula rather than an island.

In 1697, at Father Kino's urging, the Spanish government officially authorized the Jesuits to establish permanent missions in Baja California. Father Juan María Salvatierra, who was appointed superior of these missions, arrived in October 1697 to establish the first one, which would be dedicated as Nuestra Señora de Loreto (Our Lady of Loreto). It would survive for 132 years, and Loreto would soon grow into a major population center on the peninsula. Before Father Salvatierra's death in 1717, five missions had been founded in Baja California. Father Kino, meanwhile, would go on to found more than twenty missions on the mainland as far north as what is now Arizona and New Mexico.

Throughout the eighteenth century, the Jesuits gradually expanded both their spiritual and political power in New Spain. The political aspect was especially true in Baja California, where the priests would eventually create a virtual Jesuit empire. Because the harsh desert was so inhospitable, the missions were essentially the only

Father Junípero Serra

THE FOUNDER OF THE MISSION system in Alta California, Father Junípero Serra served as its father-president for fifteen years, during which time nine of the twenty-one missions were established. An unassuming man, he stood just five feet two inches tall and is said to have weighed just 120 pounds. Despite this, he would carry an enormous weight on his small shoulders.

Born Miguel José Serra at Petra on the island of Majorca on November 24, 1713, he entered the Franciscan Order in September 1730 and received his doctorate in theology from Lullian University at Palma, where he went on to serve on the faculty of the philosophy department until 1749, when he was sent to New Spain to join the faculty of the missionary college of San Fernando on the first day of 1750.

While traveling from Vera Cruz to Mexico City, he suffered an injury to his leg that would make walking difficult for the rest of his life. Despite this, Father Serra would later walk hundreds, if not thousands, of miles in the course of his work, especially after he was posted to Alta California. During his two decades in New Spain, Father Serra served as a missionary in many remote corners of the land, including the rugged Sierra Gorda north of Querétaro. While here, he mastered the language of the native people of the region and translated religious texts so that they could read them. After serving briefly as father-president of the former Jesuit missions in Baja California, Father Serra traveled to Alta California in 1769 to take up the post of father-president there. He passed away on August 28, 1784, and was buried at Mission San Carlos Borromeo de Carmelo.

After California achieved statehood in 1850, Father Serra remained as one of California's favorite founding fathers. When the United States Congress invited the states to provide a pair of statues of prominent citizens to be placed in Statuary Hall in the United States Capitol building, Father Serra was chosen for recognition. Ettore Cadorin rendered him in bronze, and this statue was installed in 1931.

There is a movement within the Catholic Church to have Father Serra canonized as a saint. In 1985, Pope John Paul II took the first step, declaring him as venerable, and in 1988 he was beatified. This second step toward sainthood was in acknowledgment of his courageousness during the early years of the development of the Alta California mission system.

Spanish settlements, so the Jesuits naturally wielded the only political power. This power would eventually lead to a confrontation with King Carlos III. In 1765, the king assigned José de Gálvez as his inspector-general for New Spain, specifically instructing him to curb the power of the Jesuits. In 1767, the Jesuits were ordered to leave New Spain permanently, and the Franciscans of the Apostolic Missionary College of San Fernando in Mexico City were asked to take over the Baja California missions. Whereas the Jesuit missionaries had come to wield political and economic power, the activities of the Franciscans would be specifically restricted to the spiritual.

Gálvez sent Gaspar de Portolá to Baja California to deal with the Jesuits there. Portolá did everything in his power to ease the transition and to make sure that what little property the missions had would not be looted. The Jesuits departed from Loreto in February 1768, and the Franciscans arrived there two months later on Good Friday. Leading them was a veteran Franciscan missionary named Father Junípero Serra. He had been in New Spain since 1749 and had served as a missionary in some of the most remote corners of the mainland before coming to Baja California.

The Franciscan experience in Baja California would, however, be short-lived. Another transfer of the Baja California missions was in the works. In 1768, Father Juan Pedro de Iriarte, the vicar-general of the Dominican Order, requested permission from King Carlos III to establish Dominican missions in Baja California that would be in addition to the Jesuit missions then being transferred to the Franciscans. When this permission was granted in 1770, the Franciscans proposed that the Dominicans simply take over the Jesuit missions as well. Those familiar with the lay of the land on the peninsula would have realized that Baja California was simply too remote and too sparsely populated to support two parallel chains of missions. Besides, Father Serra now had an even more ambitious project on his plate.

José de Gálvez had arrived at Loreto in the summer of 1768, with a mandate from King Carlos III to start establishing both missions and military outposts in Alta California. Spain had claimed the region, but beyond the voyages of Cabrillo and Vizcaíno, nothing had been done to either explore or occupy the area. It was time for this to change. To carry out the Gálvez mandate, Father Serra and Gaspar de Portolá worked out an initial plan to establish both missions and presidios, or military posts, in Alta California. Using the maps sketched by Cabrillo and Vizcaíno, they chose to establish such outposts at both San Diego and Monterey Bay.

As Father Serra and Gaspar de Portolá headed north on their new adventure, the Franciscans prepared for the transfer of the Jesuit missions to the Dominicans, a process that would be completed by 1773.

MOVING INTO ALTA CALIFORNIA

THE MOVE TO ESTABLISH A Spanish presence in Alta California proceeded like a multi-pronged military operation. Indeed, it *was* a military operation. It was under the command of Gaspar de Portolá and manned by soldiers—with the missionaries simply a small part of the deployment. Supplies were assembled in Baja California and prepared to be sent into the distant land where only a handful of Spaniards had ever set foot. Food and religious supplies were earmarked to go by ship, while livestock and bulkier items would

travel overland from Loreto in two separate groups traveling about six weeks apart. The latter of these would include Portolá, who had been appointed as governor, and Father Junípero Serra, the father-president of the new chain of missions that would take shape over the coming years in Alta California.

In January 1769, the ship *San Carlos* departed La Paz, followed a month later by the *San Antonio*, sailing from Cabo San Lucas. Neither would reach Alta California until April. A third ship, the *San José*, departed from New Spain later in the spring, but it would be lost at sea.

By July 1769, the surviving ships and the overland parties had reached their destination at San Diego. By the end of the year, Portolá had continued on as far north as San Francisco Bay. The Spanish had arrived in Alta California to stay.

Over the coming four years, four missions would be established in Alta California. As noted above, the initial mandate was to establish mis-

sions at or near San Diego Bay in the south, and Monterey Bay in the north, the two major harbors that had been explored and charted by Spanish mariners prior to the 1760s. The third mission was planned for a point that was halfway between. In fact, the third mission would be San Antonio de Padua, located much closer to Monterey Bay. The fourth mission, Mission San Luis Obispo de Tolosa, was about halfway between the first two. Four additional missions would be added during the next six years. The last mission founded under Father Serra's leadership would be Mission San Buenaventura in 1782.

AFTER FATHER JUNÍPERO SERRA

FATHER SERRA PASSED AWAY IN 1784 while waiting for the long-delayed permission to dedicate Mission Santa Bárbara. After Father Serra's death in August of that year, Father Francisco Palóu would serve as acting father-president for about a

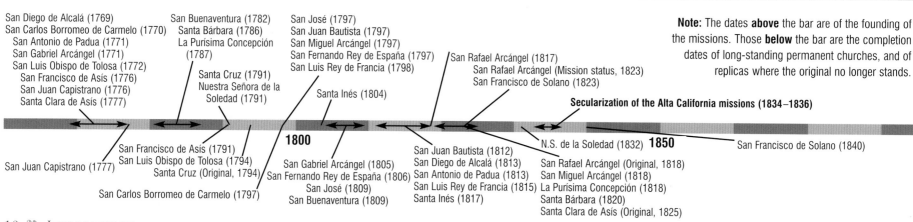

San Diego de Alcalá (1769)
San Carlos Borromeo de Carmelo (1770)
San Antonio de Padua (1771)
San Gabriel Arcángel (1771)
San Luis Obispo de Tolosa (1772)
San Francisco de Asís (1776)
San Juan Capistrano (1776)
Santa Clara de Asís (1777)

San Buenaventura (1782)
Santa Bárbara (1786)
La Purísima Concepción (1787)

Santa Cruz (1791)
Nuestra Señora de la Soledad (1791)

San José (1797)
San Juan Bautista (1797)
San Miguel Arcángel (1797)
San Fernando Rey de España (1797)
San Luis Rey de Francia (1798)

Santa Inés (1804)

San Rafael Arcángel (1817)
San Rafael Arcángel (Mission status, 1823)
San Francisco de Solano (1823)

Note: The dates **above** the bar are of the founding of the missions. Those **below** the bar are the completion dates of long-standing permanent churches, and of replicas where the original no longer stands.

Secularization of the Alta California missions (1834–1836)

1800

San Francisco de Asís (1791)
San Luis Obispo de Tolosa (1794)
Santa Cruz (Original, 1794)

San Juan Capistrano (1777)

San Carlos Borromeo de Carmelo (1797)

San Gabriel Arcángel (1805)
San Fernando Rey de España (1806)
San José (1809)
San Buenaventura (1809)

San Juan Bautista (1812)
San Diego de Alcalá (1813)
San Antonio de Padua (1813)
San Luis Rey de Francia (1815)
Santa Inés (1817)

San Rafael Arcángel (Original, 1818)
San Miguel Arcángel (1818)
La Purísima Concepción (1818)
Santa Bárbara (1820)
Santa Clara de Asís (Original, 1825)

N.S. de la Soledad (1832) **1850**

San Francisco de Solano (1840)

year. Like Father Serra, Father Palóu was born in Majorca. He was born on January 22, 1723, and joined the Franciscan Order at the age of sixteen. He studied with Father Serra and was ordained in 1743. He served as a lector at Lullian University in Palma, and came to New Spain six years later with Father Serra to a similar post at the College of San Fernando in Mexico City. He served as father-president of the Baja California missions when Father Serra went north in 1769.

When the Baja California missions were turned over to the Dominicans, Father Palóu came to Alta California, where he made several trips to northern Alta California with Gaspar de Portolá. He surveyed a number of sites for future missions and dedicated Mission San Francisco de Asís. He was at Father Serra's side when he died and remained at Mission San Carlos Borromeo de Carmelo to act as father-president until Father Fermín Lasuén assumed the post in 1785. Father Palóu returned to New Spain later that year, where he wrote a

WHO ARE THE FRANCISCANS?

The Franciscans are the Roman Catholic priests and brothers of the Order of Friars Minor, founded by St. Francis of Assisi in 1209. One of the Catholic Church's most beloved saints, St. Francis was born at Assisi in the Italian region of Umbria in 1181 or 1182, and he died there on October 3, 1226. The son of a wealthy merchant, he undertook a military career at the age of about twenty, but a few years later, he took a vow of poverty and went on to form three related Franciscan religious orders for those who joined him in a life of poverty and good works. He adopted the brown robe and rope belt as a symbol of poverty, and this became the uniform of the Franciscans, including those who came to Alta California to found the missions. The brown robes still distinguish Franciscans today.

The three Franciscan Orders were the Friars Minor, the Poor Ladies or Clares, and the Brothers and Sisters of Penance. The Friars Minor date from 1209, when Francis obtained an official sanction for the order from Pope Innocent III. The Poor Ladies began in 1212, the year that St. Clare (Santa Clara) asked Francis for permission to adopt the lifestyle of the Friars Minors. He established a convent for her and her followers at St. Damian's near Assisi. The third order was created by Francis for laypeople who wanted to follow the lifestyle without joining the cloister. The term "Franciscan" is used to identify the members of the various groups who follow the rules set out by St. Francis.

By 1211 Francis had acquired a permanent base of operations near Assisi through the generosity of the Benedictine fathers at Monte Subasio, who gave them the chapel of St. Mary of the Angels, known as the Porziuncola. By 1217, Francis had followers in Tuscany, Lombardy, and Provence, as well as in Spain and Germany.

In 1224, as he prayed on the Monte della Verna, Francis is said to have received the stigmata, meaning that he miraculously received the wounds inflicted upon Jesus Christ at the Crucifixion. Francis is said to have been the first person to have had such an experience, and his stigmata is the only one that is noted liturgically by the Catholic Church. Francis was canonized two years after his death by his patron and friend, Pope Gregory IX.

Today the Franciscans are the second-largest order within the Catholic Church after the Society of Jesus, or Jesuits.

THE MISSION TIME LINE

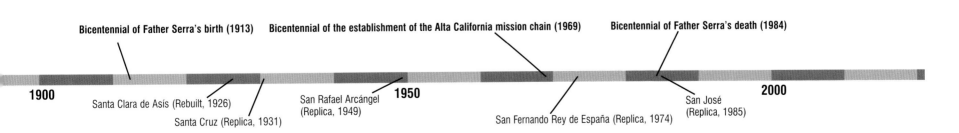

Bicentennial of Father Serra's birth (1913)   Bicentennial of the establishment of the Alta California mission chain (1969)   Bicentennial of Father Serra's death (1984)

1900   1950   2000

Santa Clara de Asís (Rebuilt, 1926)   San Rafael Arcángel (Replica, 1949)   San José (Replica, 1985)

Santa Cruz (Replica, 1931)   San Fernando Rey de España (Replica, 1974)

Above: Clay roof tiles stockpiled in a field at Mission San Antonio de Padua. Tile roofs became standard at the missions during the 1790s.
Opposite: The vividly colorful campanario, or bell tower, at Mission La Purísima Concepción.

with organizing agriculture at the missions so that they could be more or less self-sustaining. When he passed away in 1803, he had doubled the size of the Alta California chain begun by Father Serra. Like Father Serra, Father Lasuén would be buried at Mission San Carlos Borromeo de Carmelo.

A PORTRAIT OF THE MISSION

WITH A FEW EXCEPTIONS, THE missions were generally the same in their design and layout. Temporary wooden structures with thatched roofs would be replaced as soon as possible by brick or adobe buildings. A few churches would be built using stone. The permanent churches were usually begun within a year of the mission being founded, and they usually took several years to complete. In many cases, the permanent buildings were damaged and replaced. In most cases, they would be extensively remodeled several times through the years. In the early days, the roofs of the masonry buildings would be thatched, but in 1790 clay tiles were introduced at Mission San Luis Obispo de Tolosa, and within a short time they were the standard at all the missions.

Though they were the focal point of the mission, the mission church was only one of many structures that were built. These were usually built as a quadrangle, with a large plaza in the middle and the church incorporated as one part of the quad-

biography of Father Serra that was published in 1787. He also wrote what is considered by many historians to be the definitive work on the history of Alta California though 1784. Father Palóu was named as superior at the College of San Fernando, where he passed away on April 6, 1789.

Father Fermín Lasuén, who took up the reins of the Alta California mission system in 1785, was born in Victoria in Spain on June 7, 1736. Having been ordained as a Franciscan, he arrived in New Spain in 1759.

After serving briefly in the Baja California missions, Father Lasuén came north to serve at several of the Alta California missions before being named father-president in 1785. Father Lasuén continued to add to the chain of missions begun by Father Serra. Including Santa Bárbara, he would establish three missions in the space of five years.

In 1797, he began the project of systematically filling in the remaining spaces in the mission chain. He moved quickly, establishing an unprecedented

four missions during the summer of 1797 and adding a fifth in 1798. When this was done, he had accomplished his goal of placing the missions so that they were literally a day's ride apart along El Camino Reál.

Father Lasuén was also responsible for defining what we know today as "mission style" architecture. The permanent churches at most of the missions established before he became father-president were under construction during his nearly two decades in office. Father Lasuén is also credited rangle at its corner. Usually attached to the church was the convento, which housed the living quarters for the priests, as well as the mission offices. Usually there were two priests assigned to each mission, although there would sometimes be just one, and at some of the busier missions, there might be more than two.

The quadrangle also included dormitories for the neophytes, including the monjerío, where young, unmarried teenage and preteen girls, as well as widows, lived under the supervision of a matron. The other buildings included the likes of storerooms, carpenter shops, blacksmith shops, and stables. Granaries were considered to be very important, and they are frequently mentioned in surviving records from the missions.

The neophytes living on site at the mission received rations and were allowed to supplement this with the types of wild food that they had gathered before the arrival of the missions. Each neophyte was given a wool blanket and a modest clothing allowance.

Much of what the mission needed in the way of manufactured goods—including clothing, shoes, and furniture—could be produced on site, but some things would always need to be imported. These included tools, porcelain ware, fine cloth, utensils, and the mission's bells. These goods were often taken in trade for commodities made at the mission, such as candles, soap, and leather goods. Other supplies were purchased for

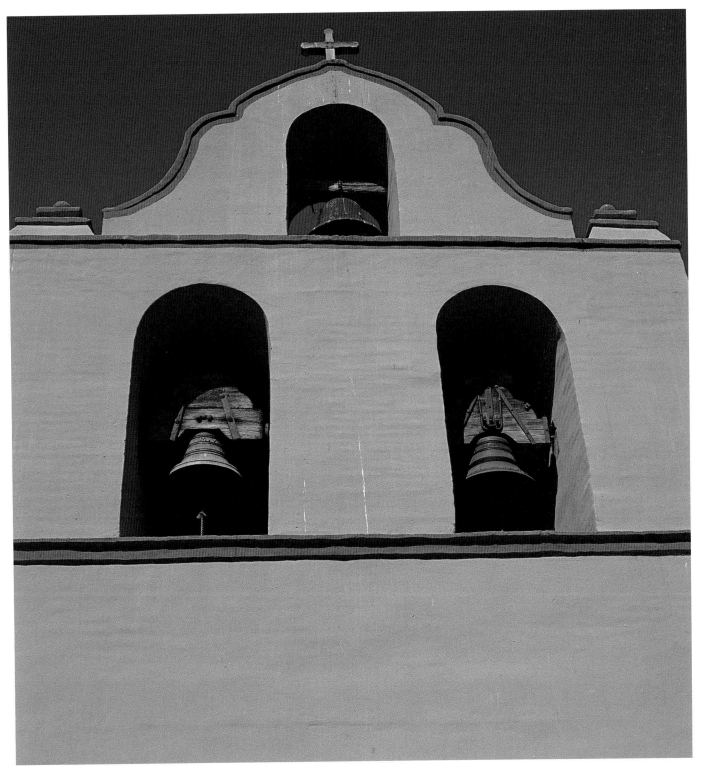

cash. This form of financial support came from the Spanish government and from the Pious Fund, a pool of money that was donated by wealthy families in Spain to further the work of the missions. Doled out annually, this fund often exceeded the government support.

Immediately outside the quadrangle would be the lavandería, or laundry facility, and workshops such as the weavery for cloth making, and the tannery, which was used for processing animal hides into leather. The barracks for Spanish soldiers were often, although not always, located outside the quadrangle. The missions were usually located adjacent to previously existing Indian villages, but as the numbers of neophytes grew, housing complexes for the neophytes were usually built nearby. In some cases, such as at Santa Bárbara, these neophyte villages covered an area more than twice as large as the quadrangle.

Missions were usually located near streams, and aqueduct and dam systems were usually constructed in order to provide the water needed by the people in the mission complex. Also located on the streams would be water-powered gristmills for grinding grain into flour.

The lands beyond the quadrangle were as essential to the survival of the mission as were the facilities contained within it. Frequently, the mission land grants encompassed dozens or even hundreds of square miles of land. This was used for the agricultural activities that allowed the missions to have the potential to be self-sustaining, and to have goods for trade with other missions and with the Spanish settlements, or pueblos, that grew up in California during the mission period. We use the word "potential" because the missions were not always self-sustaining. They occasionally suffered droughts, floods, and other hardships. It is interesting to note, however, that as hard as things were at times, none of the missions were abandoned because of natural disaster or environmental difficulties until after 1834.

Land use varied as one moved outward from the mission. Closest to the missions would be the orchards, vegetable gardens, and vineyards. Orchard crops included fruit and olives. In the southern areas, citrus was common. Indeed, the missionaries introduced citrus and many other fruit types into California. The fruit trees and vineyards grew from root stock brought in from Europe. The most important vegetable crops were peas, lentils, and beans, including garbanzos. Farther out from the mission, often many miles away, would be the fields of grain, including barley, corn, and wheat. More of the latter was grown than any other crop.

Also farther from the missions, often as far as twenty-five miles or more, were the ranchos where the livestock was kept. Horses, mules, and donkeys were in corrals close to the mission complex, but cattle and sheep were kept at the more distant ranchos. The inventory of cattle and sheep was quite large, while only a handful of goats and pigs were typically present at the missions. In addition to meat and dairy products, the cattle provided leather, which was widely used at the missions for everything from shoes to thongs for strapping beams together in roof construction. The sheep, of course, provided wool for blankets and clothing. Another by-product was tallow, which was used for both candles and soap.

In many cases, the missions built permanent settlements on the ranchos. In some cases, chapels would be constructed at these locations, and these were often used as satellite missions, known as asistencias.

CALIFORNIA'S NATIVE PEOPLES

THE FRANCISCANS WERE THE FIRST Europeans to have extensive contact with the native people of California. Far from being a single homogenous population, these indigenous people comprised many distinct groups, more widely varied than in any other state.

Linguists distinguish these groups by their language groupings. Typically, more than one tribe or linguistic group would be represented at a single mission, but the predominant native population would be the one that had lived in the area prior to the founding of the mission. In the south, near Mission San Diego de Alcalá and Mission San Luis Rey de Francia, were

Above: This reconstructed Chumash house is typical of those used by many coastal people. Dome-shaped, with a framework of bent tree limbs, it is covered with tule, or other reeds, woven tightly enough to be waterproof.
Opposite: The rugged old campanario at Mission San Antonio de Padua. The mission churches were typically built of brick as we see here, but most received a coat of stucco.

the Yuman people, who spoke Uto-Aztecan dialects that were similar to those spoken in Baja California. Farther north, especially in the vicinity of Mission San Gabriel Arcángel and Mission San Fernando Rey de España, were people who spoke Shoshonean languages related to those spoken in the Great Basin country to the east. The coastal missions from San Buenaventura to La Purísima Concepción, including Santa Bárbara, San Luis Obispo de Tolosa, and Santa Inés, were located in the traditional lands of the Chumash people. In the valley of the Salinas River were the Salinan peoples, who were represented at Mission San Miguel Arcángel and Mission San Antonio de Padua, as well

as at neighboring missions in smaller numbers. In the Monterey Bay area and inland were the Esselen people, who occupied a relatively small region that encompassed Mission San Carlos Borromeo de Carmelo and Mission Nuestra Señora de la Soledad.

North of Monterey Bay were the family of peoples who the Spanish referred to as Los Costanos, or "the Coastal People," because they lived along the Pacific Coast as well as on the shores of San Francisco Bay. Anthropologists now refer to this family as Costanoan. These people include the Ohlone family who lived in the vicinity of Mission San Francisco de Asís, Mission Santa Clara de Asís, and Mission San José. The latter mission,

and all of the inland missions in the costal valleys to the south, such as Mission San Luis Obispo de Tolosa and Mission San Miguel Arcángel, also had contact with the Yokuts people who lived to the east. Their traditional lands were centered in the San Joaquin Valley and the foothills of the Sierra Nevada beyond. They were often referred to as Tulare by the Spanish because they lived near Tulare Lake, a vast shallow lake that once existed in the vicinity of the present central California city of the same name.

Above San Francisco Bay, the missions were located in the territory of the tribes that are associated with the northern part of the state, including the Pomo, Wappo, and Wintun. Also in this area were the Coast Miwok, one branch of a people that occupied lands north of San Francisco Bay from the Pacific Ocean to the Sierra Nevada.

In general, all of the people who occupied the area where the California missions were located were what anthropologists call hunter-gatherers. They hunted small game and they gathered berries and nuts, especially acorns. The acorns were a staple food throughout Alta California. They were ground into meal through the use of a mortar and pestle and were cooked into a mush or baked into flat bread. The game that was hunted varied from place to place and from season to season, depending on what was available. Deer and rabbits were generally plentiful, as were game birds such as quail. The buffalo or bison, which were the staple meat source for the Plains Indians, were not present in California.

People living near coastal estuaries, such as near Monterey Bay and San Francisco Bay, availed themselves of the shellfish that were plentiful there. The Chumash built large ocean-going dugout canoes and plank boats, through the use of which they mastered the art of deep sea fishing. Fish such as salmon were a major part of their diet. They also used their large boats to establish villages on the Santa Barbara Channel Islands of San Miguel, Santa Rosa, and Santa Cruz.

Most of the California people lived in domed or conical houses made of tule reeds or similar material. In the case of the domed houses, the frame was often of willow, with the tule meticulously woven into it. Many of the peoples of California also mastered the art of weaving baskets. Many were elaborately decorated, and they were typically woven well enough that they were watertight.

The missionaries changed the way of life for the native peoples in many ways. The Franciscans taught them agriculture, which fundamentally changed the culture of the former hunter-gatherers. The neophytes also learned many other aspects of European culture, from trades and crafts to music and the Spanish language. Conversely, many of the Franciscans made it a point to learn the local languages and customs.

Much has been said of the negative impact that the missionaries had on the indigenous people of California. However, the intentions of most missionaries, but certainly not all, was generally benevolent. The Franciscans even went out of their way to try to shield the neophytes under their charge from the frequently abusive Spanish troops and civilians. The missionaries truly believed that they were doing the right thing by bringing Christianity and trade skills to the Indians. If anything, the missionaries can be faulted for their paternalism toward the neophytes, but this was benign compared to what many native people in the Western Hemisphere experienced from Europeans. It can be said that many indigenous people were able to adapt more easily to the arrival of European culture because of skills they learned from the missionaries.

THE MISSIONS MATURE

THE FIRST DECADE OR SO OF THE nineteenth century was a golden age for the missions of Alta California. By the time that Father Lasuén passed away in 1803, the mission system had reached maturity. As noted above, they were now roughly a day's ride apart along El Camino Reál, and most had been in operation long enough that their infrastructure was in place and activities had become routine. The orchards, vineyards, and fields had matured, and most missions were self-sustaining, either through the fruits of their own fields or through trade. Supplies also continued to flow from Spain by way of New Spain, or from New Spain directly.

Father Lasuén was succeeded as father-president of the mission system in 1803 by Father Estévan Tápis. Born in 1756 in Colona de Farnes in the Spanish province of Catalonia, he entered the Franciscan Order in 1778 and traveled to the Western Hemisphere eight years later. He arrived in Alta California by way of Monterey in 1790. His first assignment was to Mission San Luis Obispo de Tolosa, and from there he was posted to Mission Santa Bárbara. As father-president, he founded Mission Santa Inés in 1804. In 1812, he retired to Mission San Juan Bautista and was replaced by Father José Francisco de Paula Señan. At San Juan Bautista, Father Tápis pursued a love of music and developed a method of notation

Above: Father Serra established what was perhaps the first library in California at his headquarters at Mission San Carlos in Carmel. His successors added to the collection, which may have contained 2,000 volumes by 1820. This is a re-creation of how it may have appeared. Opposite: The neophyte cemetery at Mission San Carlos Borromeo. The graves are real, but the surface appearance was recently reconstructed as a Boy Scout project. Each grave is marked by an abalone shell and a cross.

to be used to teach neophytes to sing in a choir. This is discussed further in the section on San Juan Bautista. Father Tápis passed away at San Juan Bautista on November 3, 1825.

Like Father Tápis, his successor was a Catalonian. Born in Barcelona in March 1760, Father Señan was ordained as a Franciscan missionary priest in 1784 and had reached Alta

California by 1789. He served two terms as father-president of the mission system, the first between 1812 and 1815 and the second from 1820 until his death on August 24, 1823.

Serving as father-president in the interim of Father Señan's two terms was Father Mariano Payeras. Born on the island of Majorca in 1769, he arrived in Alta California at the age of

twenty-seven. During his career, he served at San Antonio de Padua, Nuestra Señora de la Soledad, and San Carlos Borromeo. His last posting was to La Purísima Concepción, where he served for a decade before becoming father-president. He would spend his final years at La Purísima Concepción, which is where he passed away on April 28, 1823.

Above: The familiar life-size bronze statues of Father Serra that are located at each of the twenty-one missions, as well as other locations, were donated by William Hannon, a Southern California real estate developer known for his generosity to the Catholic community. Hannon started the popular tradition of rubbing the statue's toe for good luck. Born in 1913, the bicentennial of Father Serra's birth, Hannon passed away in 1999. Opposite: The morning sun casts dappled shadows on the San Luis Obispo church.

THE END OF THE MISSION SYSTEM

THE BEGINNING OF THE END OF the mission era in Alta California essentially came after Mexico had declared its independence from Spain in 1821. By 1822, the full effects were being felt in Alta California. The Spanish settlements there were essentially orphaned. The missions were generally left to fend for themselves without supplies from the outside. The Mexican army would replace the Spanish at the California presidios, but the Mexican government showed little interest in continuing the support that the Spanish monarchy had provided for the missions. In fact, this support had already begun to dwindle during the years between 1808 and 1814, when Spain was distracted by the war with Napoleon.

In the wake of Mexican independence, the mission system did continue to function. After his death in 1823, Father Tápis was succeeded briefly as father-president by Father Vicente Francisco de Sarría, who in turn was succeeded by Father Narciso Durán, who would serve three terms: from 1824 to 1827, from 1830 to 1838, and from 1844 until his death in 1846. A Catalonian born in 1776, he came to the Western Hemisphere at the age of twenty-seven and he arrived in Alta California three years later. In 1806, Father Durán was posted to Mission San José, where he would spend the next twenty-seven years, including his terms as father-president. Like Father Tápis, Father Durán loved music and created a notation system for teaching neophyte choirs to sing. This activity is discussed in detail in the section on Mission San José.

In 1833, the Mexican government began a series of initiatives to shake up, and then dismantle, the Alta California mission system. The first step was what was known as the Spanish exclusion policy. Though the mission system had been founded by missionaries from the College of San Fernando in Mexico City, they were all Spanish-born. When he began his two-year term as governor of Alta California in 1833, José Figueroa decided to shake things up at the missions by replacing the priests at all of the missions north of Mission San Antonio de Padua with Mexican-born Franciscan priests from the College of Guadalupe de Zacatecas. When he arrived in Monterey to assume his new post, he brought a number of Zacatecans with him. Father Durán reacted to this turn of events by relocating the headquarters of the Alta California mission system from Mission San Carlos Borromeo de Carmelo to Mission Santa Bárbara in 1833.

It should be noted parenthetically that the Zacatecan Franciscans, along with Franciscans from the College of Santa Cruz de Querétaro, were responsible for founding most of the missions in Texas.

Meanwhile, another blow awaited the missions. Also in 1833, the Mexican congress passed the Secularization Act, which called for stripping all of the missions—from the Californias to Texas—of their agricultural lands, leaving them only their quadrangles, and in some cases, only their churches. The mission churches and attached structures would be allowed to remain as parish churches—if they could survive as such. Those which were located in or near growing cities could and often did survive. However, missions such as San Antonio de Padua and La Purísima Concepción, which were essentially in the middle of nowhere, would not.

The Secularization Act, which was ratified in 1834, essentially marked the end of the mission system as it had existed in Alta California for more than half a century.

THE AFTERMATH OF SECULARIZATION

THE FORMER MISSION PROPERTY was sold by the government or disposed of in the form of land grants to private individuals. In many cases, to the surprise of no one, these individuals were friends of government officials, or government officials themselves. In the case of Texas, these land grants formed the basis of the great cattle ranches that would figure so prominently in that state's history later in the nineteenth century. In Alta California, secularization had been marketed as providing freedom for the neophytes. However, many of them had lived within the structure of the mission system all their lives, and they found it difficult or even impossible to get by without the structure. It was especially hard to manage when the agricultural land had been handed to large land owners. Many neophytes wound up as farmhands on the former mission land, but some would continue to live near the mission quadrangles for years.

Beginning in 1840, the surviving former mission churches were placed under the management of the first bishop of the Californias, Father Francisco Garcia Diego y Moreño. Born in the Mexican state of Jalisco in 1785, Father Diego had become a Franciscan at the missionary college of Guadalupe de Zacatecas in 1801. He had first come to Alta California in 1833 with the Zacatecan priests who arrived to take over the northern missions on the eve of secularization. Basing himself at Mission Santa Clara de Asís, Father Diego had served as the administrator for the Zacatecan missions through 1835. With secularization, Father Diego had proposed that the Mexican government recommend the appointment of a bishop for California. Pope Gregory XVI finally authorized this in April 1840, and the job was assigned to Father Diego. The newly minted bishop set up his first headquarters in San Diego in 1841, but moved to Mission Santa Bárbara in January 1842. Coincidently, Father-

President Narciso Durán also had his office here, and the two men shared space until 1846, when they both passed away.

It was in 1846 that the final blow would befall the former missions of Alta California. During the previous year, Pío de Jesus Pico had begun a two-year term as the last Mexican governor of Alta California. Born at Mission San Gabriel Arcángel in 1801, he was a deal maker, gambler, and politician who had served twenty days as governor a decade earlier. He took office against the backdrop of a groundswell of support within Alta California for secession from Mexico and annexation with the United States. Knowing that the end was near, Pico decided to take secularization to its final conclusion—and to make a little money for himself in the process.

As noted above, when the missions had been stripped of their lands, the churches and adjacent buildings had remained as the property of the Catholic Church. Pico decided to move quickly to sell these and whatever was left, much of it to friends and family. In some cases, he would be closing deals for the sale of churches just a matter of weeks before the Americans arrived in the summer of 1846.

In September 1850, California became the thirty-first state in the United States. Three months earlier, Father Joseph Sadoc Alemany had arrived in the territory to assume the role of bishop of Monterey.

Above: An old mission bell at La Purísima Concepción.

A Spanish-born Dominican priest, Bishop Alemany had previously served in Ohio, Kentucky, and Tennessee. At the time that he arrived, the Diocese of Monterey was the single Catholic diocese for the entire state. Within a few years, it had been elevated to archdiocese status with three dioceses under it. In 1853, Father Alemany was promoted to archbishop of California and transferred to San Francisco.

During his early years in California, Bishop Alemany had taken an interest in the old mission churches that had been secularized, sold, and allowed to deteriorate. In 1855, he decided to pursue a claim against what he saw as the illegal seizure of mission property by the Mexican government. In 1855, his claim was upheld by the United States Lands Commission, and eventually by the United States

Supreme Court. Between 1858 and 1863, Presidents James Buchanan and Abraham Lincoln, acting on congressional authorization, formally returned the mission churches and some of the mission lands to the Catholic Church under the trusteeship of Bishop Alemany.

He also pursued a claim over Pious Fund money belonging to the missions that had been taken by the Mexican government. The case went all the way to the International Board of Arbitration in The Hague, where Bishop Alemany prevailed.

RESTORING THE MISSIONS

TODAY, ALL OF THE MISSIONS ARE owned and operated by the Catholic Church, except Mission La Purísima Concepción and Mission San Francisco Solano, which are owned and operated by the California Department of Parks and Recreation as State Historic Parks. Four missions are still operated by the Franciscan Order that founded the mission chain: San Antonio de Padua, Santa Bárbara, San Miguel Arcángel, and San Luis Rey de Francia. All of the mission churches have been restored or reconstructed to more or less their appearance during the mission period except Mission Nuestra Señora de la Soledad, where only a small chapel exists, and Mission Santa Cruz, where the replica church was built at half scale. At Mission San Juan Capistrano, the Great Stone Church has lain in ruins since the earthquake of 1812, but the little chapel that preceded it still stands and still serves as the mission church.

The details of the architectural restorations are discussed in the individual sections, but worth a mention here are two organizations who were responsible for vital stabilization and preservation work in the early days of the twentieth century. These were the California Historic Landmarks League and the Landmarks Club of Southern California. Under the leadership of Joseph Knowland, the former would be responsible for a great deal of work at San Antonio de Padua San Carlos Borromeo de Carmelo and San Francisco Solano. Founded in 1897 by Charles Fletcher Lummis, the Landmarks Club of Southern California helped to preserve and restore Mission San Juan Capistrano, Mission San Fernando Rey de España, and the San Antonio de Pala Asistencia that had been part of Mission San Luis Rey de Francia.

Born in 1859 in Lynn, Massachusetts, Lummis was quite an amazing individual. He attended Harvard and worked as a newspaper editor in Chillicothe, Ohio. In 1884, Lummis traveled to Los Angeles—on foot. During his walk, he became interested in the Southwest and its indigenous people. He would later return to the area, where he would work to promote the preservation of their rapidly fading way of life. In Los Angeles, he worked as city editor of the *Los Angeles Times*, and as city librar-

ian. He also started a magazine called *Land of Sunshine* to promote Southern California. Through the Landmarks Club, he accomplished a great deal for the old missions in an era before the public fascination with them had reached the level that it would later in the twentieth century. He would observe that the mission system had been "the most just, humane, and equitable system ever devised for the treatment of an aboriginal people." His home is now the headquarters for the Historical Society of Southern California.

It was also around the turn of the century that a woman named Anna Pitcher, who was the director of the Pasadena Art Exhibition Association, took it upon herself to revive interest in El Camino Reál. Roads following the original route existed, but the designation had been lost and forgotten. After failing in 1892 to get the Women's Club of Los Angeles to support her efforts, Ms. Pitcher succeeded with the California Federation of Women's Clubs and the Native Daughters of the Golden West in 1902. Working with Mrs. A. S. C. Forbes and Caroline Olney of the latter organization, she formed the El Camino Reál Association in 1904.

The idea was to redesignate the route as El Camino Reál, using eleven-foot markers with signs and cast-iron bells. Between 1906 and 1915, 158 markers were installed. Unfortunately, without proper maintenance, they deteriorated or were

stolen. Between 1926 and 1931, the California State Automobile Association and the Automobile Club of Southern California—who then were responsible for maintaining all the state's highway markers—took charge of the bell sign program. By 1949, the auto clubs had replaced and added bells and there were nearly 300. When the California Department of Transportation (Caltrans) took over responsibility for signage, the bells were orphaned again until 1974, when the state legislature put Caltrans in charge. They were then restored and maintained in the counties of Los Angeles, Ventura, San Benito, Monterey, San Luis Obispo, Santa Bárbara, San Mateo, and Santa Clara. In 1996, Keith Robinson, the statewide coordinator of the Caltrans Adopt-a-Highway Program, came up with an "Adopt-a-Bell" program. By the turn of the century, more than 380 bells were installed and adopted by such entities as the auto clubs and the California Federation of Women's Clubs. In October 1997, a bell marker was installed at Loreto in Baja California, which was the site of the first successful mission to be founded in the Californias, and hence the origin of El Camino Reál.

Traditionally, U.S. Highway 101 has been identified as being synonymous with El Camino Reál, and this is generally true for Mission San Rafael Arcángel, as well as seven of the ten missions from San Buenaventura to San Juan Bautista. To the south, El

Camino Reál runs on a myriad of thoroughfares. Many mission towns have streets named El Camino Reál, but in San Diego it is Mission Road that passes the mission. Northward from Mission Santa Clara de Asís, the street formally named El Camino Reál is also designated as State Route 82. In the city of San Francisco, it is Dolores Street. In October 2001, the California State Assembly formally identified El Camino Reál as "state highway routes embracing portions of I-280, Route 82, Route 238, U.S. 101, I-5, Route 72, Route 12, Route 37, Route 121, Route 87, Route 162, Route 185, Route 92, and Route 123 and connecting city streets and county roads thereto, and extending in a continuous route from Sonoma southerly to the international border and near the route historically known as El Camino Reál shall be known and designated as 'El Camino Reál.'"

Today, the preserved and restored missions are among the most important historical and cultural icons within the state of California. Each year, thousands of tourists set out to "do the missions," and an equally large number of California fourth-graders and their families travel El Camino Reál, visiting missions and discovering their state and its heritage along the way.

The idea behind the missions had been religious, and their beginning had been as political as it was spiritual. However, the most important lasting legacy of the missions has been cultural.

CHAPTER ONE

MISSION SAN DIEGO DE ALCALÁ

THE IDEA OF ESTABLISHING A chain of missions in Alta California was first realized at Mission San Diego de Alcalá. It is the anchor in the chain of twenty-one missions in California. It is both the most southern and the first to have been established. However, the story of European interest in San Diego predates the founding of the mission by more than two centuries.

If things had unfolded as they had begun, San Diego would be called San Miguel. The leader of the first European known to have made landfall in what is now San Diego was Juan Rodríguez Cabrillo, who set foot on the shores of San Diego Bay in 1542. It was standard procedure for Spanish explorers to name their discoveries after the saint whose feast day was closest to the date of discovery, so it was named San Miguel.

Many years later, in 1602, an expedition under the command of Sebastián Vizcaíno, another Spanish explorer, returned to the place that Cabrillo had called San Miguel.

Vizcaíno arrived aboard a vessel named *San Diego* and he arrived near the feast day of San Diego de Alcalá—or St. Didacus of Alcalá—so he renamed the site after this coincidence. This time, the name would be permanent.

St. Didacus was born in 1400 near Seville in Andalusia. He joined the Franciscan Order and became a missionary to the people of the Canary Islands. He later headed the infirmary at the Ara Caeli Friary in Rome, where he is said to have cured a number of people through miraculous cures. He moved to the university city of Alcalá in Spain in 1450, and passed away there in 1463. After his death, Spain's King Philip II successfully solicited for his canonization.

Though the early explorers had reported an excellent natural harbor at San Diego, it would be another 167 years before Spain decided to establish a settlement here. In 1769, the expeditions that would establish Alta California's first missions reached San Diego. First to arrive were the vessels

Above: The garden courtyard at Mission San Diego, with the statue of St. Joseph.
Opposite: The distinctive campanario at Mission San Diego. The largest bell in the campanario is the 1,200-pound Mater Dolorosa, which was cast in San Diego in 1894.

San Carlos and *San Antonio*, which landed at San Diego in April 1769. Two overland expeditions reached San Diego in June 1769 with livestock, heavy equipment, and tools. Arriving with the second overland party, headed by future governor Gaspar de Portolá, was Father Junípero Serra himself.

The overland trip had been extremely difficult, and many of the expedition members had died during the trip. However, the situation in San

Above: The fountain is located in the patio at the center of what was the quadrangle at Mission San Diego de Alcalá.

Antonio, loaded with supplies that were intended to be deposited at Monterey in preparation for the establishment of the second mission.

The *San Antonio* had not planned to stop at San Diego, but shortly after passing, it lost an anchor and the captain doubled back. The ship made an unplanned landing at San Diego, thus saving the mission there, as well as the grand plan to establish missions in Alta California.

Soon, the first temporary buildings were constructed at San Diego, and attempts were made to begin farming and to make contact with the native people of the area.

The indigenous people living in what is now San Diego County, who called themselves Kumeyaay, were members of what is now classified as the Yuman ethnic group because the languages that they spoke were part of the Uto-Aztecan linguistic group known as Yuman. All of the Kumeyaay people in the area had a similar culture, but spoke a different Yuman dialect. The largest group, those living in what is now southern San Diego County, were called Tipai, while those who lived farther north were the Ipai. The Spanish referred to the Tipai and Ipai as the Diegueño, meaning that they lived near Mission San Diego. The Kamimia, who lived farther inland, were called Cupeño by the Spanish.

Culturally, these people were what anthropologists call hunter-gatherers. They hunted wild game,

Diego was even worse. Father Serra discovered that those who had arrived by sea were sick with scurvy and many had died. Indeed, he wrote that only two men who had been aboard the *San Carlos* would survive. Including a ship lost at sea, more than a hundred people—over half the total that had started out—would perish before the initial Spanish garrison was constructed.

On July 16, 1769, Father Serra officially founded Mission San Diego de Alcalá near the initial landing site

and about six miles west of the present mission. Known as Presidio Hill because it was where the Spanish also built their military post for San Diego, the place that Father Serra picked for the mission overlooked San Diego Bay and what is now known as Old Town San Diego.

As Portolá departed to conduct an expedition into the north in search of Monterey Bay, Father Serra went to work on the new mission. Because of sickness and food shortages, things did

not go well for the San Diego settlement. When Portolá returned that winter, the people at the mission were on the edge of starvation. The ships had gone back to the port of San Blas for supplies, but they had not yet returned. Father Serra and Portolá waited through the winter. Finally, Portolá decided that they would pack up everything and return to Baja California if help did not arrive by March 19, 1770. At almost the last moment, a ship was sighted in the distance. It was the *San*

Above: The reredos above the altar was installed in the twentieth century.
Right: The statue of Father Serra at Mission San Diego de Alcalá.

Contact Information:
MISSION SAN DIEGO DE ALCALÁ
10818 San Diego Mission Road
San Diego, CA 92108-2429

Parish Office: (619) 283-7319
Visitor Center Museum
and Gift Shop: (619) 281-8449
Fax: (619) 283-7762
Library/Archives: (619) 283-6338
Tours: (858) 565-9077

Web site:
www.missionsandiego.com
E-mail:
info@missionsandiego.com

including quail, deer, and rabbits, and they gathered the acorns that are abundant throughout the region. They did no farming until shown how by the Spanish. They lived in huts made of branches and brush that were clustered into villages near the streams that flowed through the valleys. As with the native peoples throughout California, they were adept at making intricate baskets.

The initial contact between the Spanish and the native people was not especially amiable. Theft and violence ran both ways, and the mutual suspicion made the mission's task of ministering to the Kumeyaay a difficult one. At the same time, the Franciscans at the mission were discovering that their original choice of a location was not conducive to growing crops, nor was there an adequate water supply.

After five seasons of trying to make the original site work, Father Luis Jayme asked Father Serra for permission to relocate the mission. In August 1774, with Father Serra's endorsement, Mission San Diego was moved to the present site, six miles up the San Diego River into what is now known as Mission Valley, where fresh water was more easily obtained and where the mission would be closer to the Diegueño villages. There was also more space at the new site for the neophytes who had joined the mission during the first five years.

It was also in 1774 that Father Jayme officially succeeded Father Serra

as senior missionary at Mission San Diego. As father-president of the chain of missions, which numbered five by this time, Father Serra was necessarily spending most of his time elsewhere. Under Father Jayme, work began on wooden, thatched roof structures at the new site.

In those first five years, fewer than a hundred Kumeyaay had become neophytes, and relations between the mission and the Kumeyaay community at large were never good. During the summer of 1775, Father Jayme and Father Vicente Fuster began a major outreach program, which resulted in nearly 400 Kumeyaay being baptized. For many Kumeyaay, however, the efforts by the missionaries resulted in increased resentment. The Kumeyaay shamans were especially concerned with the religion of the missionaries, and this clash of cultures resulted in increased tensions. At the same time, the behavior of the Spanish soldiers and civilians at the presidio was causing increasing antagonism among the local people. Naturally, the Kumeyaay tended to lump all of the Spanish together, and the misdeeds of one group reflected poorly on the other.

Finally, around midnight on November 4–5, 1775, the animosity boiled over into a full-scale uprising. A group of Kumeyaay, which Father Francisco Palóu later estimated at about 800, attacked Mission San Diego, setting fire to the wooden and thatched structures. There had been smaller incidents previously, but this large-scale attack was the most serious that had yet occurred. Father Jayme intervened to try to stop the violence, but he was dragged down and beaten to death. He thus became the first Catholic martyr in California.

A blacksmith named José Arroyo and a carpenter named Urselino were also killed, and the mission facilities were burned to the ground. The Spanish military authorities at the presidio drew up plans for a punitive strike against the Kumeyaay, but Father Serra opposed the idea of indiscriminate reprisals against Kumeyaay villages. Ultimately, the Spanish troops concentrated on the recovery of religious items stolen from Mission San Diego in the raid, and on arresting specific instigators of the uprising. Even then, Father Serra sought pardons for those Kumeyaay that were taken into custody.

Father Fermín Lasuén was appointed almost immediately to succeed the martyred Father Jayme as senior missionary at Mission San Diego, and Father Serra arrived from Carmel in July 1776. He would remain until December to oversee the efforts that were being made to start rebuilding California's first mission at the Mission Valley site.

Constructed of brick and adobe between 1776 and 1780, the new Mission San Diego church and other structures were much more substantial than the earlier buildings, and laid out with a fully enclosed quadrangle. They were built to survive a repeat of the

Above: The reconstructed convento at Mission San Diego now houses the visitor center and museum. Opposite: The main entrance to the mission gardens. Today, visitors enjoy roses and other flowers. Once the missionaries cultivated an olive grove and vegetable gardens.

1775 incident, but there would never be another major attack. Though the relations between the missionaries and the Kumeyaay would not be marred by serious violence after 1775, the two sides would never enjoy the same cordial bond that was experienced at most of the other missions in the north.

Through the next two decades, Mission San Diego expanded. By the end of eighteenth century, the Franciscans were growing barley, corn, and wheat, as well as beans and vegetables. Grapes were being grown and wine was being made. They ran more than 1,200 head of horses and 10,000 head of cattle, as well as about 20,000 sheep on more than eighty square miles in the hills above Mission Valley.

In 1797, the mission reached its peak number of 565 baptisms.

Father Lasuén remained as senior missionary at Mission San Diego until 1785, when he assumed the presidency of the mission chain upon the death of Father Serra in 1784. Father Lasuén left San Diego for Carmel in November 1785 shortly after Father Juan Mariner arrived to take his place. In turn, Father Mariner would serve as senior missionary until his death at the mission in January 1800. He was assisted by Father José Panella and Father José Barona, who arrived in 1797 and 1798, respectively. Panella was later reprimanded by

Above: The St. Francis Wishing Well at Mission San Diego. Opposite: The main entrance to the sacristy is located adjacent to the garden.

in Spain in 1770, a year after Mission San Diego was founded, Father Martín was highly regarded as both a priest and senior missionary. He would serve for nearly two decades, until his death at the mission in October 1838.

During Father Martín's tenure, the new mission church was dedicated on November 12, 1813, the feast day of San Diego de Alcalá. Five years later, in 1818, Father Martín also oversaw the establishment of the Santa Ysabel Asistencia in the mountains sixty miles inland from Mission San Diego.

After Mexico declared its independence from Spain in 1821, the support that the Spanish monarchy had given to the missions evaporated, and Mission San Diego was compelled to become fully self-sufficient. With secularization, control of the mission lands passed from the Franciscans to the local representatives of the Mexican government. All that remained for Father Martín's missionaries was contained within their quadrangle. Through the end of 1832, a total of 6,522 baptisms and 1,794 weddings had been performed at the mission.

When Father Martín passed away in 1838, he was succeeded by Father Vicente Pasqual Oliva, who had first arrived as a priest at Mission San Diego in 1820. Father Oliva would remain until August 1846, when the Franciscans formally abandoned Mission San Diego and he moved on to Mission San Luis Rey. Ironically, the

Father Lasuén for his mistreatment of Kumeyaay neophytes and sent home in 1803. Father Barona, on the other hand, would remain and in 1800 he would succeed Father Mariner as the senior missionary at Mission San Diego and serve until 1811.

During Father Barona's term as senior missionary, work was begun on rebuilding and enlarging the mission church. It was seen as being too small to accommodate the growing population of Mission San Diego, and it had probably suffered some damage in the earthquake of 1803. The rebuilding process at the church would take until 1813. In the meantime, in 1807 the missionaries and neophytes began work on a dam upriver from the mission. This project, which would not be completed until 1816, also included an aqueduct to bring water from the reservoir to the mission complex.

In 1811, Father Barona was succeeded as senior missionary by Father Fernando Martín. Born in Robledillo

only residents of the mission were now a few Kumeyaay people who stayed on after the last Franciscans departed.

In 1848, two years after the American flag was first raised over San Francisco, California officially became a territory of the United States. During that same year, what had been Mission San Diego was leased to a rancher named Philip Crosthwaite. Two years later, the U.S. Army took over the former mission as well as former Spanish and Mexican military facilities in San Diego County. At the mission, various artillery and cavalry units would use the old church as a horse barn or storage facility until about 1859.

In 1862, the United States government officially returned ownership of Mission San Diego to the Catholic church. It was used only sporadically until well into the twentieth century, except for the period between 1892 and 1909, when the Sisters of St. Joseph of Carondolet used the site as an Indian school.

In 1931, an ambitious project was undertaken to restore Mission San Diego. It was an enormous task, because by this time nearly everything but the facade of the mission church lay in piles of rubble. After reconstruction, the church and portions of the rebuilt monastery were reopened. In 1976, Pope Paul VI designated Mission San Diego as a minor basilica. Today, California's first mission is an active Catholic parish.

CHAPTER TWO
MISSION SAN CARLOS BORROMEO DE CARMELO

T HE SECOND IN THE MISSION chain, Mission San Carlos Borromeo de Carmelo was founded in Monterey by Father Junípero Serra more than 400 difficult miles north of the first at San Diego. As had been the case with San Diego, Monterey and its bay were first charted by Europeans in 1542 during the voyage of Juan Rodríguez Cabrillo. It was probably not revisited by the Spanish until the 1602 expedition of Sebastián Vizcaíno, but the English seaman Sir Francis Drake probably passed this way in 1579.

Though it would take the Spanish 167 years to get back, Vizcaíno's description of Monterey Bay loomed large in the imagination of those planning the chain of Alta California missions.

Even before the establishment of Mission San Diego, the long-range plan called for the second mission to be at Monterey Bay, with others in between. In July 1769, almost immediately after dropping Father Serra and the others at San Diego, Gaspar de Portolá headed north with the goal of rediscovering Monterey Bay. With him was the Franciscan friar Father Juan Crespí, whose diary of the Portolá expedition still stands as an important document in early California history.

Portolá's overland expedition found Monterey Bay and even planted a cross without realizing that it was the same location described by Vizcaíno. They traveled north to San Francisco, then turned back to San Diego when they began to run out of supplies. Coincidently, it was while he was traveling back to San Diego that Portolá identified the locations where Father Serra would later establish Mission San Antonio de Padua and Mission San Luis Obispo de Tolosa.

When Portolá reached San Diego in January 1770, he considered the notion of postponing the establishment of an outpost in the Monterey Bay area indefinitely. Mission San Diego was short of food, and there were certainly not sufficient supplies to support both that mission and the

Above: The ruined mission church at Carmel, as it appeared in about 1870.
Opposite: Restored in the early twentieth century, the church now appears as it did in 1797.

expedition to establish another mission 400 miles farther north. Father Serra protested the idea of a postponement even as Portolá was preparing to return south to Baja California. Finally, the supplies arrived and the project was back in the works.

In May 1770, with Father Crespí again part of the expedition, Portolá set out again for Monterey. Father Serra, meanwhile, was ready to go north to establish the second mission, but he chose to make the trip by sea aboard the *San Antonio*. Both parties

Above: The facade and campanario still stood when this photograph was taken in about 1860, but the roof had collapsed on the mission church and the adjacent buildings were in ruins. Today, homes and trees cover the barren hillside.
Opposite: A view of the mission courtyard with the fountain in the foreground.

Contact Information:
MISSION SAN CARLOS BORROMEO DE CARMELO
3080 Rio Road
Carmel, CA 93923

Phone: (831) 624-1271
Museum Store: (831) 624-3600
Fax: (831) 624-0658

Web site:
www.carmelmission.org

would arrive at Monterey Bay by the first of June. This time, Portolá was able to ascertain that the spot that he had visited the year before was, in fact, the place where Vizcaíno had made landfall 168 years earlier. This was important, because this site had been predetermined as the location for the mission when Father Serra began the task of establishing the mission chain.

On June 3, 1770, less than a week after the expedition set foot on the Monterey shoreline, and less than eleven months after he had founded Mission San Diego, Father Serra formally established his mission. He called it Mission San Carlos Borromeo, naming it for St. Carlo (Charles) Borromeo. Born in the Italian city of

Arona in 1538, Carlo Borromeo was the nephew of Giovanni de Medici, who became Pope Paul IV in 1559. Father Borromeo served as papal secretary of state and as archbishop of Milan. He died in 1584 and was canonized in 1610.

The specific location of Father Serra's new mission was near El Estero, the lake in the center of the modern city of Monterey. It was described in contemporary accounts as being "two gunshots from the beach," or about a mile from where the Portolá expedition made landfall. A colorful legend, which probably cannot be verified, is that the mission was founded on the same spot, and under the same oak tree where the Carmelites traveling with Sebastián

Vizcaíno had said Mass more than a century before.

With a mission having been founded, Portolá established a presidio nearby and sailed away, leaving Lieutenant Pedro Fages in charge. Despite having formally established the mission in such an auspicious place, Father Serra began having second thoughts about the planned location almost immediately. As had been the case in San Diego, the mission was sited in a place that was really ill-suited for an agricultural settlement. There was also the issue of Fages meddling in mission affairs and of his troops mistreating and frightening the native Esselen people to whom Father Serra was there to minister.

Father Serra and Father Crespí scouted the area and located a better site, the present site, five miles south near the Carmel River at the mouth of the Carmel Valley. Here there was plenty of fresh water, and there was land nearby that would be suitable for cultivation and for grazing livestock. Carmel Valley was also home to a number of Esselen people, who typically made their homes in the river valleys around and south of Monterey Bay.

When the *San Antonio* set sail from Monterey on July 9, 1770, it carried a letter from Father Serra to his superiors requesting permission to relocate the mission. Nevertheless, Father Serra had begun work on a temporary wood-and-thatch church at the Vizcaíno location near where the Spanish presidio would be established.

Above: When the roof of the mission church collapsed in 1851, the nave remained open to the elements for more than three decades. A steeply peaked wood-frame roof was added in 1884, and replaced by an architecturally accurate tile roof in 1936.

Ten months later, Father Serra received a formal authorization to relocate the mission, and during the summer of 1771, Spanish workmen and neophytes from Baja California began construction on the first buildings at Mission San Carlos Borromeo de Carmelo. The church that Father Serra had built at the original site in Monterey would become the chapel for the Spanish Presidio of Monterey. It would be called La Capilla Reál, or Royal Chapel. A church in the familiar mission architectural style would be constructed on the site and dedi-

cated by Father Fermín Lasuén in 1794. Formally designated as San Carlos Cathedral in 1850, the building still exists and is still in use. It is the smallest Catholic cathedral in the United States.

Across the hills in Carmel, the first wooden church at Mission San Carlos Borromeo de Carmelo was completed to a sufficient degree that Father Serra was able to say the first Mass on the site on August 24, 1771. Exactly four months later, on Christmas Eve, Father Serra formally took up residence at Mission San

Carlos Borromeo de Carmelo, declaring it as his headquarters for the entire California mission system. By the end of 1771, the population at the mission in Carmel stood at thirty-seven, including twenty-two recently baptized Esselen neophytes.

For the rest of their lives, both Father Serra and Father Crespí would be based at Mission San Carlos Borromeo de Carmelo, although Father Serra spent a great deal of time on the road. The road was, of course, El Camino Reál, and his task was the establishment of additional missions. He founded both San Antonio de Padua and San Gabriel Arcángel in 1771, and added San Luis Obispo de Tolosa the following year.

In 1775, King Carlos III decided to make Monterey the capital of Alta California, with Don Antonio Bucareli as governor and viceroy. While Father Serra got along with Bucareli, he was at odds with other Spanish officials, such as Commandant-General Teodoro de Croix and Captain Fernando de Rivera, who were more interested in the establishment of a Spanish political and economic power in Alta California than in ministering to the spiritual and temporal needs of the native population.

After returning in 1774 from a long trip to Mexico that took more than a year, Father Serra went back to work on the project of setting up missions along the Royal Highway. By 1782, the Alta California mission system contained nine missions.

It was on January 1, 1782, that Father Serra's friend and colleague, Father Crespí, passed away at Mission San Carlos Borromeo de Carmelo. By now, Father Serra himself was in ill health. He had put in more than five decades of hard work, including more than a decade in Alta California. In his sixties, he had been on the go constantly, his days marked by back-breaking work and long overland journeys, often by foot. He turned seventy in 1783, and spent most of his final year at Mission San Carlos Borromeo de Carmelo. When the end seemed near, he sent for Father Francisco Palóu, the senior missionary at Mission San Francisco de Asís, who arrived to be with him at the end.

When Father Serra passed away at Mission San Carlos Borromeo de Carmelo on August 28, 1784, a salute was fired by a Spanish ship in Monterey Bay and bells were rung, both at the mission and in Monterey. Many people came to the mission to pay their respects as Father Serra was buried in the sanctuary, near Father Crespí, near the altar of the mission church. With Father Serra's passing, Father Palóu assumed the role of interim father-president of the Alta California mission chain until Father Fermín Lasuén arrived at Mission San Carlos Borromeo de Carmelo to assume the post on a permanent basis.

During the first two decades that Mission San Carlos Borromeo de Carmelo occupied its present location, no fewer than a half dozen different wood and adobe mission churches were located there. Father Serra had made plans for a permanent stone structure, but it was not until 1791 that a master mason, Manuel Ruiz, was brought in to undertake the job of designing and building such a structure. He was also assigned the same task for the presidio chapel in Monterey. The latter came first, and it was completed in 1794. Meanwhile, construction of the seventh—and present—church at Mission San Carlos Borromeo de Carmelo got underway in 1793, using sandstone that was cut in the Santa Lucia Mountains and brought in overland.

Dedicated in 1797, the church has been described as Alta California's most beautiful. Architectural historians also point out its Moorish influences, including the design of the tower and the window over the front door. However, much of the tile work that had existed within the church when Father Lasuén dedicated it has been lost over the years.

It is said that during the period of the construction of the church, Mission San Carlos Borromeo de Carmelo was at its most prosperous. According to mission records, the population of Esselen and other native people living at the church reached its peak of 927 in 1794. Compared to the more or less constant state of animosity that existed between Mission San Diego and the surrounding native population, the relations between the Franciscans at

Above: Constructed in 1957, the reredos above the altar at Carmel's mission church is based on the one at San Francisco's Mission Dolores.

Mission San Carlos Borromeo de Carmelo and the Esselen people were excellent. The missionaries taught them various agricultural and building trades, and they participated in both construction work and farming at the mission. Vineyards, as well as corn and wheat fields, were planted in the Carmel Valley, and both cattle and sheep were run on the hillsides and the surrounding area. Inside, the mission boasted a substantial library, the first institutional library in California. Having originated with Father Serra's own collection, it was added to over time and is said to have contained around 2,000 books by 1820.

Meanwhile, Father Lasuén continued Father Serra's work of founding additional missions. In the dozen years between 1786 and 1798, he added nine missions to the chain, doubling the total to eighteen. In 1797 alone, he would establish four. Of equal importance was that he oversaw construction of churches throughout the mission system, including ones at missions established by Father Serra. By the 1790s, El Camino Reál was a busy thoroughfare and supplies moved easily throughout the mission system. It was an era of prosperity for most of the missions.

Above: Much fanfare accompanied the opening of Father Serra's grave in 1882. He was disinterred to dispel concerns that his crypt had been disturbed by grave robbers during the several decades that the mission church had been abandoned and in ruins. The other graves may be those of Father Juan Crespí, Father Fermín Lasuén, or Father Julian Lopéz, all of whom are buried at the mission. The St. Patrick's School band donned their uniforms and came down from San Francisco to provide music for the occasion.
Opposite: This sarcophagus, now in the Mission San Carlos museum, was created in 1922 by sculptor Joseph Mora. It features Father Serra in repose, with Father Crespí at his head and Father Lasuén and Father Lopéz at his feet.

Like Father Serra, Father Lasuén would make his headquarters at Mission San Carlos Borromeo de Carmelo until his death, and he would be interred at the church there. He passed away on June 28, 1803, at the age of sixty-seven.

During the early years of the nineteenth century, the Franciscans gradually expanded the physical size of Mission San Carlos Borromeo de Carmelo, even as the neophyte population began to decline. The quadrangle at the mission was finally enclosed in 1815, nearly two decades after the completion of the permanent mission church, and a mortuary chapel was constructed in 1821.

When Mexico declared its independence from Spain in 1821, the outside source of supplies for the missions dried up and the mission system gradually went into decline. Mission San Carlos Borromeo de Carmelo probably fared better than many others, but the number of neophytes is known to have decreased to just 381 by 1823. This was only about a third of the number who had been present at the turn of the century. Through the end of 1832, a total of 3,827 baptisms and 1,032 weddings had been performed at the mission.

Father José Reál became the senior missionary in 1833, one year before secularization led to the sale of all of the mission lands right up to the front door of the church itself. By 1836, Father Reál had moved to Monterey and Mission San Carlos Borromeo de Carmelo was largely abandoned. San Carlos Church in Monterey became the parish church for the parish that contained the decaying mission.

Within a decade, most of the buildings at the mission quadrangle had crumbled, and in 1851, the roof of the church itself collapsed. In 1859, nine years after California's statehood, the United States Lands Commission recommended that the property around the mission be restored to the Catholic Church, and President James Buchanan authorized that title to nine acres be transferred to the archdiocese of San Francisco, which had charge of all Catholic activities in California. The

archbishop at the time was Joseph Sadoc Alemany, who had previously served as bishop of Monterey between 1850 and 1853, and who was well aware of the mission.

Despite the change of ownership, Mission San Carlos Borromeo de Carmelo would lie in disuse and decay for another quarter-century. Mass would be said here on San Carlos Day in November, but for most of the rest of the time, the only congregation was the squirrels who inhabited the ruins in large numbers. The neglect is particularly amazing given the fact that the mortal remains of both Father Serra and Father Lasuén lay beneath the ruins. Through the years, there were rumors that Father Serra's body may have been stolen, so twice, in 1856 and in 1882, his grave in the floor of the church was opened and inspected.

The second time that Father Serra's grave was examined, it was because the location had been forgotten. So, too, had been the whereabouts of the graves of Father Crespí and Father Lasuén, as well as that of Father Julian Lopéz, a young priest who had been buried at the mission in 1797, the year that the church had been dedicated. The search was successful, and all four grave sites were found. The publicity surrounding this inquiry proved to be the catalyst for raising money for the first major restoration of the church since the mission had been abandoned a half-century earlier. Father Angelo Casanova, who served as the resident pastor in Monterey between 1870 and 1893, undertook a major effort to address the physical needs of the crumbling mission church. Father Casanova's project involved construction of a replacement for the roof that had collapsed.

On August 26, 1884, a century after Father Serra's passing, Mission San Carlos Borromeo de Carmelo was rededicated. Though the new roof was peaked and wood-shingled, not a replica of the original roof, the church was finally enclosed from the ravages of rain and wind for the first time since 1851.

Further reconstruction work was done in 1924 under the direction of Father Ramón Mestres. In this project, a section of the crumbled structures northeast of the bell tower was rebuilt. Father Mestres also placed the bodies of Fathers Serra, Lasuén, and Crespí in a bronze and marble sarcophagus that had been created in 1922 by the Spanish sculptor Joseph Mora.

Nearly a decade later, in 1931, Father Philip Scher invited San Francisco–born cabinetmaker and artist Harry Downie to undertake additional restoration work at the mission. Downie arrived in Carmel for a project that might have taken a year or two, but he became so deeply engrossed in Mission San Carlos Borromeo de Carmelo that he would remain with the project for nearly half a century, until his death at the age of seventy-seven in 1980.

Downie carefully researched the mission documents and faithfully followed the original intentions of the mission builders in planning his reconstruction. One of his first efforts was the replacement of the architecturally inaccurate roof with one that was like the 1797 original. After World War II, Downie would also be called upon to supervise and consult on restoration work being done at other missions, notably Mission San Antonio de Padua.

Throughout the later twentieth century, the long-neglected Mission San Carlos Borromeo de Carmelo gradually regained the importance that it deserved as having been the original headquarters of the California mission chain. In 1961, San Carlos Borromeo de Carmelo was elevated to the status of a minor basilica by Pope John XXIII. In August 1984, to mark the bicentennial of Father Serra's death, the bishops of California gathered at the mission. Coincidently, it was on this occasion that San Carlos Borromeo de Carmelo's original fountain was returned to the mission after having been taken from the ruins more than a century earlier.

Above: Just beyond the fountain is the building that Harry Downie used as a workshop during his half-century of work at the mission. It now houses historical exhibits. Downie arrived in 1931 and remained there for most of the rest of his life.
Below: The final resting places of Harry Downie and his wife, adjacent to the shady north side of the church in the mission cemetery.
Opposite: Bougainvillaea drapes a portion of the restored convento that now houses the mission museum.

In 1933, two years after Harry Downie came to the mission, Michael O'Connell became the first full-time pastor at Mission San Carlos Borromeo de Carmelo in almost a century. Father O'Connell would collaborate with Downie on the enormous task of returning the old mission to as close an approximation as possible to that which was present when Father Lasuén dedicated the mission church in 1797.

Three years later, in September 1987, Pope John Paul II paid a visit to Mission San Carlos Borromeo de Carmelo as part of his papal tour of the United States. It was the ultimate tribute that could be paid to this humble little mission that had once stood alone so far from the centers of power within the church.

CHAPTER THREE

MISSION SAN ANTONIO DE PADUA

WHEN THE EXPEDITION LED by Gaspar de Portolá traveled north from San Diego on their overland journey toward Monterey Bay late in 1769, it passed through the Santa Lucia Mountains, about a day's ride south of Monterey. Portolá made a note of a particular site that he thought might make a good location for a mission. There was abundant water in the rolling, oak-covered hills, and it looked like just what he thought the Franciscan missionaries would find appropriate.

When Portolá met Father Junípero Serra in Monterey, he briefed him on this place that he called the Valle de los Robles—the Valley of the Oaks. Father Serra was intrigued and checked the site for himself. Portolá was right. Though the location of the present Mission San Buenaventura had been planned as the third mission location in the Alta California system, Father Serra decided to make the Santa Lucia Mountains site the next mission instead.

As the story goes, Father Serra came here on July 14, 1771, and found a place near a stream that he called the River of St. Anthony. He hung a bell in an oak tree, rang it, and announced that here would be a church. The church would be Mission San Antonio de Padua, named for St. Anthony of Padua.

Born in Lisbon in 1195, Anthony was said to be a descendant of Godfrey de Bouillon, the leader of the First Crusade. A gifted scholar, he became a Franciscan friar and traveled throughout Europe. During his career, he is credited with having performed a number of important miracles. A vision of the Christ child is said to have appeared to him near the town of Camposanpiero, near Padua in Italy. He founded a convent in Padua, where he spent his final years. He died at Vercelli, also near Padua, in June 1231.

Father Serra remained in the Valley of the Oaks for about two weeks, then he returned to Mission San Carlos Borromeo de Carmelo, leaving Father Buenaventura Sitjar in

Above: The side altar at Mission San Antonio de Padua. Opposite: The bare brick facade of the mission church and the adjacent arcade approximate the appearance of the original.

charge of building the new mission. Not only would he build the mission, Father Sitjar would remain as its senior missionary until 1808—although he took time out in 1797 to serve briefly as the first administrator at nearby Mission San Miguel Arcángel.

As had been the case in both San Diego and Monterey, the first site picked for the mission was shown not to be the best. Located in a flood plain, it was prone to be inundated in the spring, but short of water in the summer, so in 1773, Mission San

permanent location, to about 1,300 in 1805.

During his nearly four decades as senior missionary at Mission San Antonio de Padua, Father Sitjar compiled one of the most important ethnographic documents to come out of California's mission period. While most Spaniards were content to teach the local people to speak to them in Spanish, Father Sitjar mastered the local Teleme dialect of the Salinan language to the extent that he was able to produce a written dictionary of the dialect. It was not, however, published in the United States until 1861. Meanwhile, at Mission San Juan Bautista, Father Felipe del Arroyo de la Cuesta had done similar work in studying and recording a Mitsun dialect that would not be fully recognized until the 1860s.

Even as a great deal of work was going into the development of infrastructure at the mission, work on the permanent mission church at San Antonio de Padua did not get underway until 1810. It would be formally dedicated three years later, in 1813. Though it was relatively far from any major settlements, Mission San Antonio de Padua had a rather robust religious community. This was probably attributable to the relatively good relations that were enjoyed with the native people. Indeed, San Antonio de Padua would record more baptisms and weddings through the end of 1832 than would Mission San Carlos Borromeo de Carmelo at

Antonio de Padua was moved farther north in the valley to the present location. A dam was constructed about three miles up the San Antonio River, and a system of reservoirs and aqueducts was built. So too was a water-powered gristmill, said to have been the first in California.

With an adequate water system, Mission San Antonio de Padua grew quickly and prospered. The climate was temperate in this location between the chilly coast and the warmer Salinas Valley to the east. Gardens, fields, and

vineyards were planted, and livestock was grazed in the surrounding hills and valleys. Records from 1774 indicate that the mission possessed seven horses and sixty-eight head of cattle. By 1805, however, the number of horses had increased to about 800, and there were 7,362 cattle and roughly 11,000 sheep at the mission.

Reportedly, relations between the Franciscans and the Salinan-speaking Teshhaya, or Mitsun, people who populated the Santa Lucia Mountains got off to a good start

and remained that way. In both San Diego and Monterey, the influence of other Spanish settlements, such as the presidios, had a negative effect on relations between the missionaries and the native people. At Mission San Antonio de Padua, there were no such distractions and the Franciscans were able to build a bond of friendship and cooperation with the Indians. The number of Salinan people living at Mission San Antonio de Padua increased from 178 in 1774, the first year after the move to the

Above: The main altar at the San Antonio de Padua mission church. Right top: The tumbled-down church and convento as they appeared in the late nineteenth century prior to the restoration efforts of Senator Joseph Knowland and the California Historic Landmarks League.
Right: This is how the altar in the mission church would have appeared in the early twentieth century. Opposite: Sunlight streams into the San Antonio mission church in this view looking into the nave from near the altar.

Contact Information:
MISSION SAN ANTONIO DE PADUA
P.O. Box 803
Jolon, CA 93928
Phone: (831) 385-4478
Fax: (831) 386-9332

resident priest until 1844, a decade after secularization. The following year, attempts were made by the Mexican government to sell the mission, but no buyer could be found and it was abandoned.

In 1853, three years after California became a state, the church assigned a priest to Mission San Antonio de Padua. Father Dorotéo Ambrís took up residence at the mission and remained until 1883. During that time, thirty-three acres of former mission land were deeded back to the Franciscan Order.

After Father Ambrís, however, no priest would be sent to remote Mission San Antonio de Padua for many years. It was considered to be simply too isolated to be worth the investment required to keep it up. The infrastructure was long overdue for proper maintenance, and with no one in residence, Mission San Antonio de Padua simply fell into ruin. Insect-riddled timbers holding the roof collapsed in 1890 and the tiles would wind up being reused in the Southern Pacific Railroad station in Burlingame, California. Some would even make their way to a Mission San Francisco de Asís restoration project.

Early in the twentieth century, a new mood of nostalgia for the old California missions came to the fore, and citizens throughout the state became interested in preserving and restoring them. In the case of Mission San Antonio de Padua, it

Carmel. There were 4,419 baptisms and 1,142 weddings at San Antonio de Padua, compared to 3,827 baptisms and 1,032 weddings at the headquarters mission at San Carlos Borromeo de Carmelo.

During the early decades of the nineteenth century, cities were gradually growing up around the Spanish missions. Indeed, many, such as those in San Diego, San Francisco, and Carmel, had been started at roughly the same time as settlements that would evolve into major cities. Mission San Antonio de Padua and Mission La Purísima Concepción were different. They each evolved in areas that remained quite isolated from other settlements. As such, the changes experienced at the time of Mexican independence and secularization were less abrupt and less dramatic. Though Mission San Antonio de Padua began a gradual decline, it would continue to have a

Above: Much of the aqueduct system constructed in the late eighteenth century by Father Sitjar is still visible in the area surrounding Mission San Antonio.
Right: A restored mill on the mission lands. The mission may have had the first gristmill in California.
Opposite: The gardens within the mission quadrangle were restored in the 1940s.

would be Senator Joseph Knowland, the leader of an organization called the California Historic Landmarks League. Beginning in 1903, this group began raising money for the reconstruction of San Antonio de Padua, which they regarded as the most picturesque of missions that survived in the northern part of the state.

The California Historic Landmarks League faced a daunting task. Repairing structures that had been in deterioration for many decades was difficult enough, but Knowland could not have predicted in 1903 the natural disasters that would lie ahead. The storms that battered the Santa Lucia Mountains in the winter of 1904–1905 dropped nearly two feet of rainfall, damaging the work already completed, as well as raising the San Antonio River to a torrent. Then, a year later, the Great Earthquake of April 18, 1906— centered north of San Francisco— caused a great deal of damage along the San Andreas Fault, which runs through the valley to the east of Mission San Antonio de Padua.

Despite the setbacks, the California Historic Landmarks League resumed their work, completely restoring the mission church at San Antonio de Padua by 1907. As had been the case at Mission San Carlos Borromeo de Carmelo, however, they reroofed the structure with a wood-shingled roof rather than a replica of the original roof completed in 1813.

In 1940, in anticipation of a possible United States entry into World War II, the United States War Department acquired more than 200,000 acres of ranch land between the Salinas Valley and the Pacific Ocean for use as a training facility. This included all the land surrounding Mission San Antonio de Padua. In 1941, this training area was designated as the Hunter Liggett Military Reservation, named for the late Lieutenant General Hunter Liggett,

Above: Mission San Antonio de Padua as seen across the poppy-covered fields to the southwest. Opposite: The old, rugged campanario at the mission church on a warm April morning.

who had commanded the First Corps of the American Expeditionary Forces during World War I.

Renamed in 1975 as the Fort Hunter Liggett Military Installation, the post is today operated primarily as the U.S. Army Reserve Command Western Reserve Training Center, which is used by both active duty and Army Reserve components.

After World War II, the Hearst Foundation became involved in donat-ing money for a new round of restora-tion work at Mission San Antonio de Padua. Indeed, William Randolph Hearst himself had once used the hills near the mission as a hunting preserve, and his legendary San Simeon estate is located only about a dozen miles as the crow flies across the mountains from San Antonio de Padua.

Begun in 1948, the new restora-tion project was under the supervision of Harry Downie, who had been doing similar work on an ongoing basis at Mission San Carlos Borromeo de Carmelo since 1931. Under Downie, the mandate was to recon-struct the mission as closely as possi-ble to the way that it would have appeared when the mission church was dedicated in 1813.

As he had done at Carmel, Downie removed the peaked, shingled roof, replacing it with a tiled one. From there, the buildings of the quad-rangle, as well as the gristmill near the river, were reconstructed with authen-tic early nineteenth-century methods and materials.

Today, the reconstructed Mission San Antonio de Padua remains as the most remote of all the California mis-sions. Though it is just a half dozen miles from the small town of Jolon, the mission is nearly thirty miles by a winding mountain road from U.S. Highway 101.

Chapter Four

Mission San Gabriel Arcángel

Mission San Gabriel Arcángel was the fourth in the Alta California mission system, founded less than two months after the third mission and just two years after the first. The new mission was dedicated to San Gabriel Arcángel, or St. Gabriel the Archangel. Recalled as the archangel of mercy, Gabriel is, along with Michael and Raphael, one of three archangels mentioned in the Bible. Ultimately, each of the three would have one of the twenty-one missions named for him.

The site had been previously surveyed and selected by Father Junípero Serra, but the mission was formally dedicated by Father Pedro Benito Cambón and Father Angel Somera on September 8, 1771, while Father Serra was still in the Monterey area. Four years later, however, Father Fermín Lasuén would move the mission five miles to the northeast to get it out of the flood plain of a seasonal streambed. Here it would remain.

The native Tongva people who lived throughout the Los Angeles Basin, from the San Gabriel Mountains to the Pacific Ocean, knew the area of the mission as Sibagna, or Tobiscagna. The language spoken by the Tongva is classed by linguists as Shoshonean, making the Tongva linguistic relatives of the Shoshone people who lived throughout the Great Basin country of what is now Nevada, Utah, and Idaho. Noted for their magnificent plank canoes, the coastal-dwelling Tongva were accomplished mariners and are recalled as having been the people who greeted Juan Rodríguez Cabrillo when he dropped anchor off what is now San Pedro in 1542. To the Spanish, the Tongva would be known as the Gabrieleño people because of the association that they would come to have with Mission San Gabriel Arcángel.

For Mission San Gabriel Arcángel, more important than the proximity to the Tongva villages would be its proximity to the Spanish pueblo about a dozen miles to the west. Officially established in 1781 as Pueblo de Nuestra Señora de los

Above: The stairway leading to the choir loft is a signature architectural feature.
Opposite: Capped buttresses and narrow windows are also unique to Mission San Gabriel.

Angeles de Porciuncula (City of Our Lady the Queen of the Angels of Porciuncula), this settlement would grow into the metropolis known today as Los Angeles, the largest city in California. Also important geographically for the growth and evolution of Mission San Gabriel Arcángel was the fact that it was on a crossroads. While the entire mission chain would be located along El Camino Reál, San Gabriel Arcángel was located at the point where this major north-south road intersected the major highway coming from the east from Santa Fe, as well as a third route coming from Mexico. Everyone traveling from Mexico or the United States, including all major traffic coming to Los Angeles, passed San Gabriel Arcángel.

Over the span of nearly two decades, a series of mission churches were located at the site. Work on the present church, designed by Father Antonio Cruzado, began in 1791. Father Cruzado had trained as an architect at Córdoba in Spain, and the heavy buttresses used at San Gabriel Arcángel are said to be patterned after those at the cathedral in Córdoba. They were also an important practical feature for a mission located in earthquake country.

The foundations of the church and the other buildings were of fieldstones, laid in lime mortar. The walls of the church would be partly of stone and partly of brick, laid in lime mortar and thinly plastered on both sides. Unlike most mission churches,

Right: The southwest facade of Mission San Gabriel Arcángel, including the campanario, as photographed by Henry Withey in April 1937. The street has since been rerouted away from the church.

Opposite: The campanario of Mission San Gabriel Arcángel was added to the church in the 1820s, although several of these bells were present in the previous campanario that fell in the 1812 earthquake. The large bell at the lower left was cast in 1830 and was known to be audible as far away as Los Angeles during the nineteenth century. Among the other bells are three that were cast for the church in Mexico City by Paul Ruelas in 1795, and two that were cast in 1828 by Major G. H. Holbrook of Medford, Massachusetts, who is said to have learned the art of metalwork from Paul Revere. Holbrook cast the center bell and the one at the peak. The Ruelas bell at the right is dedicated to "Mary, most pure." The one at the peak was sold to the Plaza church in San Gabriel, and was rehung at the mission in 1931. The one at the left of the center row is said to have fallen in a windstorm in the 1870s and to have been missing for over half a century.

Contact Information:
MISSION SAN GABRIEL
428 South Mission Drive
San Gabriel, CA 91776-1299

Phone: (626) 457-3035
Fax: (626) 282-5308

Gift Shop/Tours:
428 Junípero Serra Drive
San Gabriel, CA 91776
(626) 457-3048

Web site:
www.sangabrielmission.org

the one at San Gabriel Arcángel had its main entrance on the side of the nave, rather than on the end. The church was originally constructed with an arched stone roof, but this was damaged in the 1803 earthquake while the church was under construction, and it was replaced the following year by a wood-frame roof with a flat wood ceiling. The roofs over the baptistery and sacristy would remain of stone laid in lime mortar.

The church was dedicated in 1806 and it remains there today. However, the original campanario on the northeast corner was destroyed in the earthquake of December 8, 1812, and replaced by the distinctive pierced wall constructed to the west of the south entrance. This structure has served as the Mission San Gabriel Arcángel campanario ever since.

Most of the growth and development of Mission San Gabriel Arcángel during the early nineteenth century was attributable to the energetic Father José Zalvidea, who served as senior missionary for two decades, beginning with the initial completion of the mission church. He oversaw reconstruction after the 1812 earthquake and a systematic expansion of agricultural production at San Gabriel Arcángel.

As might be expected of a mission on the outskirts of Los Angeles that sat astride three major highways, Mission San Gabriel Arcángel came to play an important role in the economic and cultural life of the southern part of Alta California. Thanks in no small measure to the work of Father Zalvidea, the mission would rank as the number one agricultural

OPEN FIREPLACES

AFTER THE KITCHEN WAS DESTROYED BY FIRE IN 1812, OPEN FIREPLACES WERE BUILT HERE. THEY WERE DESIGNED TO HOLD IRON KETTLES IN WHICH BEEF *and* CORN (POPCORN SOUP) WERE COOKED TO FEED THE INDIANS.

THESE REPLICAS ARE SIMILAR *in* SIZE, SHAPE *and* MATERIAL TO, *and* ARE BUILT DIRECTLY OVER, THE ORIGINAL FIREPLACES.

producer among all the twenty-one missions for the fifty years from 1782 to 1832. During this period, San Gabriel Arcángel would produce 11,685 tons of vegetables and grains, including 6,386 tons of wheat. In 1832, the San Gabriel Arcángel livestock herd numbered 26,342 head, including 16,500 cattle. In terms of livestock, San Gabriel Arcángel was second only to Mission San Luis Rey with its vast cattle ranches. Mission San Gabriel Arcángel was also noted for its wine, which was traded throughout Alta California, and the mission's workshops are said to have produced most of the candles and soap products that were used throughout the mission system.

Mission San Gabriel Arcángel also had one of the largest neophyte populations of any of the missions. Through the end of 1832, a total of 7,825 baptisms were performed at the mission, more than at any other except at Mission Santa Clara de Asís. In that time, 1,916 weddings took place at San Gabriel Arcángel, making it third among the missions behind Santa Clara de Asís and San Francisco de Asís. In addition to doing most of the work in building Mission San Gabriel Arcángel, many of the Gabrieleño neophytes would be employed on various construction projects in the pueblo of Los Angeles.

In addition to the lands immediately surrounding the mission complex, San Gabriel Arcángel had operations that were a substantial distance

Above and opposite: The peaceful mission gardens and the reconstructed trellises. The marble statue of Father Serra was erected on the mission's 150th anniversary.

Above: The Campo Santo, or cemetery, at Mission San Gabriel has been in use since 1778. Among those interred here are many of the neophytes who passed away in the especially severe epidemics that are known to have occurred in 1825. Opposite: The old crucifix is the centerpiece of the Campo Santo.

away, including a cattle ranch that was more than fifty miles east near what is now Redlands in San Bernardino County. In 1810, Mission San Gabriel Arcángel established a small chapel at the ranch called San Bernardino de Siena that may have later evolved into an asistencia, or satellite mission.

The golden age of Mission San Gabriel Arcángel ended abruptly with the secularization decree in 1834. Although the Franciscans remained at the mission complex until 1852, the intricate system of fields, farms, and workshops collapsed.

An Indian attack at the San Bernardino de Siena Asistencia in 1834 marked its demise as a satellite mission. A rancher named José de Carmen Lugo acquired it in 1842 and it was later owned by Mormon immigrants for several years. It was sold to Dr. Benjamin Barton in 1857. San Bernardino County would acquire the property in 1925 and it would be restored as a historical site by 1937.

Mission San Gabriel Arcángel itself was abandoned during most of the 1850s, and is said to have been the lair of cattle thieves in and around 1856. It was reoccupied in 1859, and would serve as a parish church until 1908. In that year, the Claretian Fathers acquired the property and began restoration work. Today, Mission San Gabriel Arcángel, located in the heart of the city of the same name, is once again an active parish church.

CHAPTER FIVE

MISSION SAN LUIS OBISPO DE TOLOSA

THE SITE FOR MISSION SAN Luis Obispo de Tolosa, like that of Mission San Antonio de Padua, was identified by Gaspar de Portolá in the course of his journey north from San Diego in search of Monterey Bay in late 1769. Known as Tishlini to the native Chumash people, it was located in an oak-filled valley not far inland from the Pacific Ocean.

To Portolá's expedition, however, Tishlini would be La Cañada de los Osos, or the Valley of the Bears. How it got this name has become an important part of the folklore of San Luis Obispo de Tolosa. As the story goes, Portolá's expedition was running dangerously short of food when they happened upon the valley. Here, they discovered evidence of a large number of bears having been digging for tule roots. A hunting excursion was undertaken, and the Spaniards were soon feasting on bear meat. Three years later, when food shortages became critical at both Monterey and San Antonio de Padua, hunters were sent back to La Cañada de los Osos, and

again bear meat helped save the hungry Europeans. According to the stories, the hunting trip of 1772 netted more than four tons of dried and salted bear jerky that could be kept through the winter.

The success of the hunt also probably caused Father Junípero Serra to consider Portolá's earlier suggestion of La Cañada de los Osos as a potential mission site. Strategically, it seemed like an ideal location for the next mission, being roughly halfway between Monterey Bay and Mission San Gabriel Arcángel. Accompanied by Father José Cavaller and Captain Pedro Fages, Father Serra came here to see for himself, and he formally established Mission San Luis Obispo de Tolosa with a dedication Mass on September 1, 1772.

He named his fifth mission for St. Louis, the bishop of Toulouse in France. Born at Brignoles in Provence in 1274, Louis was the second son of Charles II of Anjou, who would later reign as king of Naples. He was also the younger brother of Charles Martel

Above: In this view from the altar at the mission church, one sees the balcony, with the pipe organ on the left and the old Spanish chandelier above the doorway. Opposite: Mission San Luis Obispo is located at the heart of the central California city of the same name.

and a nephew of St. Louis IX, the king of France. Louis was educated by Franciscans in Spain after having been captured in battle as a young man. He entered the priesthood and served in various posts before being named bishop of Toulouse in 1296 by Pope Boniface VIII. Widely admired for his compassion toward his people, as well as for his administrative skill, Louis would unfortunately not have long in

his post. He became ill during the summer of 1297 and died on August 19.

When Father Serra left for San Diego, he left Mission San Luis Obispo de Tolosa in the hands of Father Cavaller. Two neophytes and a few soldiers also remained to assist in building the first structures at the mission. Generally, the Chumash and Salinan people living in the area welcomed the mission, and relations

Above: The nave of the mission church as photographed by Henry Withey in December 1936. Above left: A statue depicting Mary, Queen of Heaven from the mission church. Opposite: The main altar at Mission San Luis Obispo as it has appeared since 1947.

Contact Information:
MISSION SAN LUIS OBISPO DE TOLOSA
Old Mission Parish
751 Palm Street
San Luis Obispo, CA 93401

Phone: (805) 781-8220
Fax: (805) 781-8214
Gift Shop Phone:
(805) 543-6850

Web site:
www.missionsanluisobispo.org
Parish Office E-mail:
office@oldmissionslo.org
Gift Shop E-mail:
info@missionsanluisobispo.org

were good. Father Cavaller began baptizing the native people, but they were not the only ones to be entered into the baptismal record. In time, more Spanish people arrived in La Cañada de los Osos to join the small community that was growing up around Mission San Luis Obispo de Tolosa. In November 1774, a young lad named Juan José Garcia became the first non-native to be baptized in Alta California. Through the end of 1832, a total of 2,644 baptisms and 763 weddings would be performed at the mission.

Despite the mission's having earned the respect of the local people, San Luis Obispo de Tolosa was not successful in establishing harmonious relations with everyone living in the rolling hills of California's central coast. The local people had enemies, and these people were antagonistic toward the mission as well. This animosity boiled over in November 1776 with the beginning of a series of assaults against the mission by people from native bands living farther south. The attackers used flaming arrows, which were fired into the

thatched roofs of the mission buildings. The wood and thatch structures burned easily and there was a great deal of damage. Fortunately, two of the buildings, the church and the granary, were saved.

The attacks at Mission San Luis Obispo de Tolosa would continue off and on through the 1780s, leading eventually to a fundamental change in the Alta California mission system, but not exactly what the attackers had intended. In 1790, the missionaries at San Luis Obispo de Tolosa decided to rebuild their structures using fired clay

roof tiles such as were used in Europe. Making the tiles was not as easy, nor as expedient, as using thatched tule, but once they were in place the clay tiles were completely fireproof, not to mention their being effective in sheltering buildings from the winter rains. The practice was quickly embraced by the builders of the other missions, and the clay tile roofs are still in evidence today.

In the meantime, the missionaries had decided to establish an asistencia, or sub-mission, near some Chumash villages located in the steep mountains about ten miles north of Mission San Luis Obispo de Tolosa. In 1787, the Santa Margarita de Cortona Asistencia was founded at Rancho de la Playa near the location of the present town of Santa Margarita.

In 1792, two decades after Mission San Luis Obispo de Tolosa was dedicated, work was finally begun on the present mission church and its campanario. Two years later, both the church and the rectory were completed—naturally, with clay tile roofs.

The golden age of the cultural and economic prominence of Mission San Luis Obispo de Tolosa can be said to have been ushered in with the arrival of a new senior missionary, Father Luis Antonio Martínez, in 1798. He would remain until 1830, as the mission developed a sprawling infrastructure of fields, orchards, and vineyards. Around the mission church and its adjacent structures, the village that would evolve into the present city

of San Luis Obispo was gradually taking shape.

It was during Father Martínez's term as senior missionary that the quadrangle was completed in 1819, and the following year, San Luis Obispo de Tolosa's famous mission bells were hung. Specifically commissioned by Father Martínez, they were cast by Manuel Vargas in Lima, Peru. The largest of these, called Angelus, weighs 1,800 pounds and hangs today in the center of the San Luis Obispo de Tolosa campanario. The smaller of the bells still hangs at the mission, but two others were damaged in transit and were recast into a single bell.

Though Father Martínez was well liked at Mission San Luis Obispo de Tolosa, he did not get along at all with the Mexican authorities who took over Alta California after Mexico declared its independence from Spain in 1821. Among other things, Father Martínez was very critical of the Mexican plan to secularize the mission system. He predicted that Alta California's native population would be worse off after such a move. He was correct, but he had been arrested and deported by Mexican Governor Echeandía four years before the secularization laws were officially enacted in 1834. Mission San Luis Obispo de Tolosa would be officially secularized the following year, and its several thousand acres of land were subdivided and sold off to friends of Mexican government officials. The Asistencia of Santa Margarita de Cortona was sold to a man named Joaquin Estrada. The church at Mission San Luis Obispo de Tolosa theoretically remained as the property of the Franciscans. Father Luis Gil y Taboada, who replaced Father Martínez in 1830, passed away in 1833 and was succeeded by Father Ramón Abella, formerly of Mission San Francisco de Asís. In turn, Father Abella died in 1842. He would be the last Franciscan to preside over Mission San Luis Obispo de Tolosa.

In 1845, Pío Pico, the last Mexican governor of Alta California, undertook his policy of seizing and selling off the last of the real estate that had once been part of the mission system. At Mission San Luis Obispo de Tolosa, the ruined structures were sold to Captain John Wilson for $510, roughly the equivalent of $12,000 in today's dollars. During the tenure of Father Martínez as senior missionary, the estimate of the total value of the mission had been roughly 140 times greater than it sold for in 1845. Through the coming years, the mission buildings would be used for various purposes. The wing to the south of the church entrance that was constructed as a convento would be used for a school, a jail, and as the first county courthouse.

In 1846, during the Mexican War, U.S. Army forces under Colonel John C. Frémont passed through the village of San Luis Obispo. At one point, they surrounded the mission church, having received reports that

Above: This view of the main altar was taken from a extra nave that was added at a right angle to the original in the nineteenth century to accommodate additional worshippers. The tabernacle is on the right. Opposite: The facade of the mission church, seen here under the shade of the surrounding eucalyptus trees, was restored to its original appearance in 1934.

Mexican troops were holed up there. It turned out to be a small number of frightened civilians. Frémont later used the church to try a local man, coincidentally named Pico (probably no relation to the former governor), for treason. The guilty verdict was subsequently overturned. Meanwhile, Frémont is said to have also detained and released Joaquin Estrada.

Under a decree signed by President James Buchanan in 1859, a number of the mission churches—or what remained of them—were returned to the Catholic Church. Among these was Mission San Luis Obispo de Tolosa. Coincidently, the city of San Luis Obispo was officially incorporated in 1859.

Having suffered the ravages of neglect, the mission church would suffer again as a result of earthquakes that occurred during the middle of the nineteenth century, especially in 1868.

Meanwhile, possession of the former Santa Margarita de Cortona Asistencia passed to Martin and Mary Murphy of San José in 1861. Today it remains in private hands as part of Rancho Santa Margarita. Part of the original stone structure forms the foundation of a barn.

In 1880, a major renovation was underway at Mission San Luis Obispo. The objective at that time was not restoration of the mission church as it has appeared in 1794, but rather to remodel it as a functional modern—and usable—parish church. In 1880,

this involved a new, wood-shingle roof, as well as construction of a wood-frame, New England–style steeple. The adobe walls were even cased in white-washed wood planking. In 1893, Father Valentin Aguilere constructed an addition to the north side of the sanctuary. With its new look, Mission San Luis Obispo de Tolosa would serve its parishioners well into the twentieth century.

Ironically, the church at the mission where clay tile roofs were first used in California would have a wooden roof for four decades. This came to a disastrous conclusion in 1920, when a fire struck Mission San Luis Obispo de Tolosa. Once again, a tile roof was installed. In 1926, the parish centered at the mission church opened its Mission Central High School, which is now known as Mission College Preparatory School.

By the 1930s, there was a growing nostalgia throughout California for the old missions as they had originally appeared. In 1933, when Father John Harnett became the pastor at Mission San Luis Obispo de Tolosa, he took the first steps toward an authentic restoration of the church. Under his direction, the wood siding was stripped off and the steeple dating back to 1880 was taken down.

Father Harnett also oversaw the reconstruction of the narthex and belfry. Though his mandate was to make them look as they had a century before, he had the foresight to use earthquake-resistant reinforced con-

Above: The arcade in the mission gardens is covered with wine grapes. The Franciscan missionaries planted the first vines here in the eighteenth century. Opposite: The restored convento adjacent to the mission church houses the museum and gift shop, as well as the parish hall for the Mission San Luis Obispo Parish.

crete rather than the brick and mortar used in the original.

Further renovation work was begun in 1949 under the guidance of Harry Downie, who had been working at Mission San Carlos Borromeo de Carmelo since 1931, and at Mission San Antonio de Padua since 1948. Among the projects undertaken at San Luis Obispo de Tolosa by Harry Downie was the construction of an extension on the north side of the nave. Funded by the Hearst Foundation, this addition provided more floor space and it gave the church its unique L-shaped layout. As it has for more than a century, the old mission church at San Luis Obispo de Tolosa today serves its community as a parish church. At the beginning of the twenty-first century, the parish consisted of 2,200 families.

The city of San Luis Obispo, which grew up around the mission, became an economically important center in the region at the beginning of the twentieth century thanks in part to the arrival of the Southern Pacific Railroad in 1894. Today, the mission and the surrounding Mission Plaza sit in the heart of what is one of the most vibrant downtowns of any moderately sized California city.

CHAPTER SIX

MISSION SAN FRANCISCO DE ASÍS

WHEN GASPAR DE PORTOLÁ was on his 1769 expedition in search of Monterey Bay, he was aware of another important bay farther north. The English buccaneer explorer Sir Francis Drake had wintered at such a place in 1579, and plans had been laid for eventually establishing a mission in the vicinity of Drake's Bay.

In 1769, the area was still largely unexplored by Europeans, so Portolá was unsure of exactly what to expect. In November of that year, he found what he thought was the same bay where Drake had landed. In fact, Portolá discovered San Francisco Bay—which Drake had missed in the fog. Drake had sailed past the entrance to San Francisco Bay and had made landfall in Marin County at what is now known as Drake's Bay. He had never set foot inside the Golden Gate.

Viceroy Antonio Bucareli realized that a bay of the proportions of the one that Portolá had identified was potentially very important both as a port facility and as an outpost of the

empire. Just as the Franciscans saw the importance of establishing missions, so too did the viceroy realize the political and economic importance of settlements here. Knowing that the Russians were active in Alaska and were surveying the coast of the Pacific Northwest, the Spanish were anxious to stake their claim to Alta California as far north as practical.

In 1776, with the presidio and settlement at Monterey now firmly established, Bucareli ordered Captain Juan Bautista de Anza to go north to survey the area near the Golden Gate for both a presidio and a mission. In March of that year, Captain de Anza and a party that included Lieutenant José Joaquin Moraga traveled north, camping at a small lake near what is now the corner of Dolores Street and Eighteenth Street in the city of San Francisco. They named the area Arroyo de Nuestra Señora de los Dolores, or Valley of Our Lady of Sorrows. When they reported back to Monterey, it was decided that this spot would be a good place for the sixth in

Above: The cemetery at Mission San Francisco de Asís, with the 1791 mission church in the background and the 1926 spires of the basilica beyond. Opposite: The old mission church.

the chain of missions. The presidio would be located at a strategic location overlooking the Golden Gate so that it could guard the entrance to San Francisco Bay.

Three months later, a group of colonists and two Franciscans, Father Francisco Palóu and Father Pedro Benito Cambón, returned to the

Arroyo de Nuestra Señora de los Dolores. On June 29, Father Palóu celebrated Mass, dedicating Mission San Francisco de Asís for St. Francis of Assisi, the founder of the Franciscan Order. Though the official name of the mission would eventually become the name of the surrounding city, the mission itself would come to

be better known as Mission Dolores, after the arroyo.

While Father Palóu had founded the mission with a Mass said in June, the dedication would be officially celebrated on October 4, the feast day of St. Francis. The first such celebration was, in turn, delayed until October 9, 1776, so that Lieutenant Moraga, the newly appointed first commandant of the nearby Presidio, could be present. San Francisco's first military post would be commanded by the lieutenant until his death in 1785. His final resting place would be beneath the floor of Mission Dolores.

Father Palóu's original mission church was a small tule arbor structure located at what is now the corner of Camp and Albion streets in San Francisco, near a village occupied by members of the Yelamu branch of the Ohlone people. The Ohlone are part of the family that anthropologists now refer to as Costanoan because they dwelled along the shores of the Pacific Ocean, Monterey Bay, and San Francisco Bay. The Ohlone, living in what is now San Francisco, hunted game in the city's now-famous hills and valleys, and ate the fish and shellfish that they gathered from bay waters.

As was the case with most of the early missions, the location of the mission church would be moved from the site of the original temporary structure. In this case, the permanent site would be less than two blocks west of its forerunner on what is now Dolores Street near Sixteenth Street.

The cornerstone of the present Mission Dolores church was laid under the supervision of Father Palóu on April 25, 1782. This church, the oldest structure in San Francisco, was dedicated nine years later on April 3, 1791. Father Serra is thought to have said Mass at the mission church while it was under construction. This would make it, along with Mission San Juan Capistrano, one of only two surviving churches where he said Mass.

Made by the Ohlone neophytes of sun-dried adobe brick, the walls would be four feet thick. As determined by a National Park Service survey in the 1930s, the individual bricks were four inches deep by eight inches wide by sixteen inches long. The completed building was 110 feet long and thirty-two feet six inches wide. The original floor was made of clay, burned brick, tile, and wood. This was later replaced by concrete, except in the baptistery, where a few of the old tiles would survive. The roof trusses were hewn logs lashed together at the joints with rawhide, while the ceiling was made of hewn planks held together by wooden pegs made of native hardwoods such as madrone. The original ceiling still survives, as do the wooden trusses, although the latter were augmented by steel during Willis Polk's restoration work done in the early twentieth century. Initially, the roof of the Mission San Francisco de Asís church was thatched, but this fire-prone treatment was replaced by clay tiles

Above: The old mission church with clapboard siding applied, and with the 1876 brick and mortar church in the background. This church was destroyed in 1906. Opposite, top: An 1860s view of the old mission church and the convento. Opposite, bottom: The facade of the mission church has changed little since 1791.

Contact Information:
MISSION SAN FRANCISCO DE ASÍS (MISSION DOLORES)
Mission San Francisco de Asís
3321 Sixteenth Street
San Francisco, CA 94114
Phone: (415) 621-8203

Web site:
www.missiondolores.org

four years later, in 1795. The mission campanario has a bell cast in 1792, and two larger ones that were cast in 1797. They were probably in place by the turn of the nineteenth century.

The exquisite baroque-style reredos was brought in overland from Mexico. It was almost certainly made in Spain, and it may have been situated in a Mexican church before being brought to San Francisco. Stained and lacquered, it was finished in gold leaf, much of which still survives more than two centuries after it was installed. It retains the original pigments, stains, gold leaf, and lacquer with which it was finished. Other surviving fixtures that were installed in the mission church at the turn of the nineteenth century that survive in the twenty-first century are statues of St. Ann, St. Clare, St. Joachim, and St. Michael, as well as two statues of St. Francis.

In addition to the grave of Lieutenant José Moraga, there is a slab that covers the family crypt of José Jesus de Noe, the last Mexican alcalde, or mayor, of San Francisco. Noe's Rancho de San Miguel surrounded Mission Dolores and the heart of the ranch later evolved into Noe Valley, one of San Francisco's most desirable residential neighborhoods. A prevailing mystery that is still a topic of conversation in San Francisco is the exact whereabouts of the remains of Noe himself. He passed away in 1862, but only his wife and two of his children, who preceded him in death, are mentioned on the slab covering the family crypt. The old cemetery adjacent to the south side of the mission church is the final burial place of a number of early San Franciscans and early Californians. The oldest of the marked graves is that of Don Luis Argüello, the first governor of Alta California after Mexico became independent of Spain.

The mission quadrangle, which extended north and west of the mission church, included the area now occupied by the Mission Dolores Basilica and the parking lot of the Mission Dolores Elementary School. A convento with its roofline peaked at the same angle as that of the church was constructed north of the church and the two were connected by a block of storerooms and other facilities. The other buildings on the quadrangle contained the rectory for the two missionaries, as well as storerooms. Numerous workshops located here were used by carpenters and blacksmiths, and for other trades from soap-making to candle-making. There were two mule-powered gristmills, and a reported twenty looms for spinning wool and weaving cloth. The wool was derived from the herds of sheep that were run on nearby hillsides. The mission also maintained agricultural land farther to the south in what is now San Mateo County.

Between 1785 and the end of 1832, church records indicate that Mission Dolores raised 120,000 bushels of wheat, 70,226 bushels of barley, 18,260 bushels of corn, 14,386 bushels of beans, 7,296 bushels of peas, and 905 bushels of lentils and garbanzos. Also according to church records, the number of cattle reached a peak of 11,340 head in 1809, while the number of sheep peaked at 11,324 in 1814. The number of horses reached 1,239 in 1831 and mules numbered forty-five in 1813. By contrast, the inventory in 1832, on the eve of secularization, was estimated at 5,000 head of cattle, 3,500 sheep, 1,000 horses, and fifteen mules.

A cluster of small dwellings for the neophytes was located outside the quadrangle, although there was a dormitory for neophyte girls within the mission complex. A school was also in operation by at least 1818.

Beginning with the first baptism of an Ohlone neophyte on June 24, 1777, there would be 6,898 baptisms through the end of 1832. This placed Mission San Francisco de Asís third among the twenty-one missions behind Mission San Gabriel Arcángel and Mission Santa Clara de Asís. During that same period, there were also 2,043 marriages, more than at any other location except Mission Santa Clara de Asís, where there would be 2,498 weddings through 1832.

The church calculates that the era from about 1814 to 1824 was the period of the greatest prosperity for Mission Dolores. The neophyte population is said to have reached a peak of 1,242 in 1820. By 1828, however, the condition of the mission had declined to the point where only a single missionary would be in residence.

After the Secularization Act was ratified in 1834, the mission lands, and even some of the buildings in the mission quadrangle, were taken over by settlers and businesses. Saloons and dance halls were within shouting distance of the church door, and such activities as cockfighting and bear fighting occurred on what was once the mission grounds. The latter involved capturing wild bears and lassoing them from horseback for the amusement of spectators.

Father Miguel Muro, the last Franciscan missionary, left Mission San Francisco de Asís in October 1845, and Father Prudencio Santillan, the first non-Franciscan priest, took over the church the following year. The church would continue to serve as a parish church through most of the mid-nineteenth century. Had it not, it probably would not have survived, since it was located in a city that would experience incredible growth in the years immediately following the gold rush of 1849. While many of the buildings in the mission complex were torn down, the convento, along with the mission church, would remain.

As would be the case with many of the missions, there would be efforts made in the nineteenth century to update and modernize Mission Dolores. For example, the interior, including the woodwork, was whitewashed by well-meaning parishioners in the 1860s. Later, the whitewash was removed—by equally well-meaning parishioners—causing serious damage to the wood and the original painted artwork beneath. Also during the

1860s, part of the line of shops connecting the mission church to the convento were torn down and replaced by a two-story building constructed on the north side of the mission church to house a small seminary and a rectory.

During the 1870s, the archdiocese of San Francisco tore down the convento and erected a much larger brick church immediately adjacent to the mission church. Dedicated on July 4, 1876—the United States Centennial—it would overshadow the little mission church until the morning of April 18, 1906. The Great Earthquake of 1906 so severely damaged the brick building that it had to be pulled down. The old mission church, meanwhile, suffered no apparent serious harm.

In 1913, the archdiocese began work on a larger church to replace the brick building destroyed in the 1906 earthquake, and in 1916 Archbishop Edward Hanna contracted with noted San Francisco architect Willis Polk to undertake a restoration of the mission church itself. Polk called for a steel framework to be inserted within the building, with the work to be done without disturbing the original construction, such as the interior adobe walls, the wooden ceiling, and the roof trusses. When the work was completed, the original roof tiles were relayed, augmented by some that were taken from the then-abandoned Mission San Antonio de Padua.

Delayed briefly during World War I, the large new Mission Dolores Church, with two matching towers, opened in time to be dedicated on Christmas in 1918. In 1926 the archdiocese decided to remodel this church for the 150th anniversary of the founding of the original Mission San Francisco de Asís. The two towers, then less than eight years old, were removed and replaced by a pair of mismatched towers, one taller and one shorter than those of the 1918 church. The new towers and the entire facade were redone in a baroque variation of the mission style architecture that had been the talk of the 1916 San Diego Exposition, and which is still evident in San Diego's Balboa Park. In 1952, because of the historic importance of Mission San Francisco de Asís, the new church was officially elevated to basilica status. While the original mission church would be referred to as a chapel, the Mission Dolores Church became designated as Mission Dolores Basilica. Pope John Paul II would call on Mission Dolores in September 1987 during his papal visit to the United States.

The Mission San Francisco de Asís complex has remained relatively unchanged since 1926. While the structures survived the October 1989 Loma Prieta Earthquake, a powder-post beetle infestation in statues and other interior woodwork led to fears of irreparable damage and forced the temporary closing of the mission church during May 2000. After the beetles were eradicated, the church was reopened.

Above: The spires of the Mission Dolores Basilica rise above the old mission church. Completed in 1926, the newer building was granted basilica status in 1952.
Opposite: Sunlight washes into the rear of the nave at the mission church. The slab on the floor marks the final resting place of the wife and two children of José Jesus de Noe, the last Mexican alcalde, or mayor, of Yerba Buena, the village that became the city of San Francisco. The location of the remains of Noe himself are unknown and the object of many theories that enrich San Francisco's folklore.
Overleaf: Two views of the area near the main altar at Mission Dolores. The old reredos behind the altar was brought in from Mexico around the beginning of the nineteenth century. Also dating from this period are the carved wooden statues of St. Ann, St. Clare, St. Joachim, and St. Francis. St. Michael is at the top center of the reredos.

CHAPTER SEVEN

MISSION SAN JUAN CAPISTRANO

HROUGHOUT THE FOLKLORE that surrounds the missions of California, there is perhaps no legend quite so compelling as that of the swallows of Capistrano. Each year, thousands of cliff swallows make their nests at Mission San Juan Capistrano, and their annual spring-time arrival, on or about March 19, is a much-heralded event that has been celebrated in prose and song.

Known as the "Jewel of the Missions," Mission San Juan Capistrano is also known for the ruins of its massive stone church, which was destroyed in the Great Earthquake of 1812. The ruins, which sit silently amid beautiful gardens, have always been considered poignantly picturesque.

The mission is named for St. John of Capistrano, who was born in the Italian city of that name in 1385. He studied law in Perugia, and was appointed governor of Perugia by the king of Naples in 1412. Four years later, he was captured in the war between Perugia and the Malatesta,

and while in prison he decided to become a Franciscan friar. After taking his vows, he studied under the Franciscan theologian St. Bernardine in Siena. Beginning in 1425, he traveled throughout Italy, preaching to large crowds and developing a reputation as a healer of the sick. At the same time, he authored a number of books on the issue of heresy.

Beginning in 1439, John of Capistrano undertook a series of diplomatic missions on behalf of the pope, which took him to Milan, Burgundy, and throughout the Austrian Empire. He later accompanied a military campaign that was launched against the Turkish invaders in Hungary, and he personally led troops into battle against the Turks in the Battle of Belgrade. John of Capistrano died in October 1456 and was canonized in 1724.

The third mission in Southern California, and the seventh mission in the Alta California system, the one dedicated to St. John would have been the sixth if things had gone according

Above: This early twentieth-century postcard is typical of the memorabilia that has appeared through the years to celebrate Mission San Juan Capistrano's most illustrious visitors. Opposite: The fountain is the centerpiece of the quadrangle at the heart of the mission. The buildings in the background date from the early days of the nineteenth century.

to plan. Father Fermín Lasuén formally dedicated the site with a celebratory Mass on October 30, 1775, nearly a year before Mission San Francisco de Asís, and went to work setting up the mission.

Contact was made with the local Acjachemen people, whom the

Spanish would call Juaneño because they lived near Mission San Juan Capistrano. The Acjachemen, who spoke an Uto-Aztecan dialect that linguists call Takic, had traditionally lived in the coastal area from present-day Laguna Beach, south to San Onofre. The Acjachemen were related

Above: The campanario at Mission San Juan Capistrano contains four bells that were originally hung in the Great Stone Church. Two, named for St. Vincent and St. John, were cast in 1796, while the other two, named for St. Anthony and St. Raphael, were cast in 1804. Despite being damaged in the 1812 earthquake, they were rehung in this campanario in 1813, where they continued to toll daily through the years. In 2000, for the sake of tonal quality, it was decided to cast replicas using molds made from the original bells.

to the Takic-speaking people living near Mission San Luis Rey de Francia, who referred to themselves as Ataaxum, which meant "people," and whom the Spanish called Luiseño, after the mission. The missionaries at San Juan Capistrano got along well with the Acjachemen, but their initial collaboration was short-lived. On the night of November 4–5, 1775, less

than a week after the missionaries had set up shop, a band of Kumeyaay people attacked Mission San Diego de Alcalá, killing Father Luis Jayme and burning most of the mission buildings. When it became known that this incident was part of a general uprising in what is now San Diego County, the decision was made to abandon Mission San Juan Capistrano for the

time being. The mission bells were buried and the missionaries beat a retreat to the Presidio of San Diego. This was despite the fact that the Acjachemen people did not seem to be interested in joining the hostilities.

A year later, on October 31, 1776, Father Junípero Serra arrived back at the site of Mission San Juan Capistrano. The bells were retrieved

and hung in a tree. Father Serra said Mass on November 1, rang the bells, and rededicated the location.

Work was begun on the initial mission church almost immediately, and it was completed in 1777, with the labor being provided mainly by neophytes. Other buildings, including living quarters and storerooms, as well as blacksmith and carpenter shops, were generally constructed after 1796, with work on the quadrangle being completed in about 1806. Barracks for the Spanish soldiers who protected the mission were located outside the quadrangle.

The walls of the buildings were made of sun-dried adobe brick, with limestone lintels over some of the doors and windows. A National Park Service survey in 1937 noted that the piers and arches of the colonnades were made of brick, with sandstone stringers and keystones in the arches. All of the walls, both inside and out, were plastered and whitewashed. The roofs were originally of heavy frame construction and covered with tile. The floors were mostly of large red brick tile.

As was the case at all of the missions, the first mission church was not intended to be the permanent church. For Mission San Juan Capistrano, the Franciscans had planned what would be the largest and most elaborate church in all of Alta California. It was to be just outside the quadrangle. Construction of this large stone struc-ture began in 1796, under the direc-

Above: An excavation and partial reconstruction of the metal furnaces at Mission San Juan Capistrano.
Right: The famous Golden Altar at the old mission church. This grand seventeenth-century reredos was imported from Barcelona in 1906 for the Los Angeles cathedral, but it was never used. It was eventually brought here and installed between 1922 and 1924.

Contact Information:
MISSION SAN JUAN CAPISTRANO
Mailing Address:
P.O. Box 697
San Juan Capistrano, CA 92693
Street Address (deliveries):
31414 El Camino Reál
San Juan Capistrano, CA 92675

Phone: (949) 234-1300

Web site:
www.missionsjc.com

tion of a master stonemason who was brought in from Mexico. The materials included both blue and yellow sandstone, some of which was fieldstone, and some of which was quarried at a location about six miles from the mission. Both yellow and blue stones were used for quoin treatment of the exterior arches, cornices, moldings, and pilasters. Stone was also used for the roof, which consisted of arches and domes. Completed in 1806, the church was in the shape of a cross, 180 feet long and forty feet wide at the transept. A campanario tower that

stood the equivalent of twelve stories could be seen over a wide area.

Sadly, this magnificent church only stood for six years. On December 8, 1812, a powerful earthquake struck Alta California. It occurred on the San Andreas Fault, and was centered near the present town of Wrightwood, fifty-nine miles north of Mission San Juan Capistrano in what is now San Bernardino County. Seismologists have calculated its magnitude as 7.0 on the Richter scale. The temblor was felt as far north as the San Francisco Bay Area and it caused serious damage at

missions as far north as Mission La Purísima Concepción. The worst damage, however, was at Mission San Juan Capistrano. The huge tower fell and most of the nave collapsed. So too did the entire roof. Only the sanctuary and sacristy, where the walls were thickest, survived relatively intact. A total of forty neophytes who were in the church at the time were killed.

The original mission church, meanwhile, survived the quake in reparable condition. When the decision was made to indefinitely postpone rebuilding the Great Stone

Above: This archway is one of the few details left of the Great Stone Church that was destroyed in the 1812 earthquake. Cut from sandstone by master masons, this arch once graced the interior of the largest and grandest church in Alta California.
Opposite: An old weathered gate within the quadrangle at Mission San Juan Capistrano.

Church, the old brick and adobe structure became the permanent church at Mission San Juan Capistrano. Today it survives as the oldest active church in the state of California. It is now known as "Serra's Church" or "Serra's Chapel," because it is one of only two surviving mission churches where Father Serra is known to have said Mass. The other is Mission San Francisco de Asís, where he would have said

Mass before the present mission church was fully completed.

Despite the tragic loss of the mission's centerpiece, San Juan Capistrano continued to prosper. By the turn of the nineteenth century, a thousand neophytes were living at or near the mission, and a sprawling settlement of both Spanish and Indian families was growing up around the mission. Records show that the mission had conducted 1,649 baptisms

through 1796, and that nearly 2,700 would be performed between 1796 and the end of 1832.

The Acjachemen are said to have been well integrated into life at Mission San Juan Capistrano. In addition to having worked as laborers, they learned such trades as blacksmithing, woodworking, weaving, and leather working. They also became skilled at making such mission staples as wine and olive oil. San Juan Capistrano

became an important producer of tanned hides and tallow, which were traded with the missions to the north and to settlements throughout Alta California.

Beyond the growing settlement at Mission San Juan Capistrano, fields of barley, corn, and wheat spread out toward the pastureland where the mission grazed the livestock from which the hides and tallow were derived. In 1811, the mission's fields reached a watershed year, producing 250 tons of wheat, which was 12 percent of all the wheat produced here in the fifty years from 1782 through 1832. In addition to this, 101 tons of corn, ninety-five tons of barley, and ten tons of beans were produced in 1811. The annual average for the 1782–1832 period for all types of crops other than wheat was just 105 tons. In 1811, the mission pasturelands had about 14,000 head of cattle and 16,000 sheep. This is compared to 10,900 head of cattle and about 4,800 sheep in 1832.

One of the most perilous interludes in San Juan Capistrano history came in 1818. In the autumn of that year, the French pirate Hippolyte de Bouchard sailed from Hawaii to the coast of Alta California with an eye to do a bit of plundering on his way to Argentina. He raided Monterey and Santa Barbara, and on December 14 he reached San Juan Capistrano with his band of 350 buccaneers aboard the ships *Argentine* and *Santa Rosa*. Bouchard needed provisions for the long voyage ahead. He knew that San Diego, the next stop down the coast, was too well defended by Spanish troops, so he put an emissary ashore to demand supplies from the missionaries at San Juan Capistrano.

The impertinent people of Mission San Juan Capistrano refused his demands, so he landed about half his men and a number of cannons to take what he needed by force. Fortunately, most of the gold and valuables had been hidden by the time that the pirates manhandled their artillery up the hill to the mission, so it was not plundered. Unfortunately, the pirates found the mission's wine cellar. In the drunken melee that ensued, a number of structures surrounding the mission were sacked and burned. After four days, Bouchard's men had loaded stolen supplies of food and drink and had departed. Hardly something to have been celebrated at the time, the visit by Hippolyte de Bouchard is now considered to be one of the more colorful events in Mission San Juan Capistrano folklore. Today, San Juan Capistrano celebrates the event with its annual Pirate Festival in October, in which attendees are encouraged to dress as pirates, and prizes are given for the best costumes.

The Alta California mission system began its long decline after Mexico declared its independence and Spain withdrew its support. As the figures above indicate, Mission San Juan Capistrano had been in decline economically even before it was secular-

ized in 1834. A decade later, the mission was virtually deserted. When he became the last Mexican governor of Alta California in 1845, Pío Pico dealt the final crushing blow to the former Spanish missions. Under secularization, the mission lands were confiscated and sold, but the churches remained in religious hands. Pico's idea was to sell the churches. Mission San Juan Capistrano was sold to an Englishman named John Forster—who just happened to be Pío Pico's brother-in-law—for $710. This is the equivalent of about $15,000 in today's dollars.

During the two decades that Mission San Juan Capistrano was in private hands, there was one attempt made to restore the Great Stone Church. However, this poorly planned 1860 effort actually did more damage to the ruins. Five years later, in 1865, the mission was one of the last of the missions returned to the Catholic Church under the series of federal orders that would eventually return title to all twenty-one missions.

During the latter half of the nineteenth century, the town of San Juan Capistrano gradually evolved into

an important stage stop on the road from San Diego to Los Angeles, but it remained relatively small until the arrival of the California Central Railroad line in 1887. Walnut and orange groves were planted in the area, and the region prospered.

As would be the case at a number of the other missions early in the twentieth century, people began to take an interest in the restoration of the crumbling landmark. In the case of Mission San Juan Capistrano, it would be the Landmarks Club of Southern California, founded in 1897 by Charles

Above: Bougainvillaea and the Spanish royal flag adorn the arcade that overlooks the mission quadrangle at San Juan Capistrano. Opposite: A side chapel in the original mission church. The building is known as "Serra's Church" because it is one of just two buildings still standing where Father Serra said Mass. The other, at Mission Dolores in San Francisco, was not yet complete when he visited.

Fletcher Lummis. This organization undertook fundraising activities, and they hired Los Angeles architect A. B. Benton to oversee an effort to stabilize the mission.

When Father John O'Sullivan became the pastor in 1910, he energetically pursued further restoration efforts despite his having been diagnosed with tuberculosis. The mission and the pastor developed a symbiotic relationship in which, as O'Sullivan worked to restore the mission, it seemed to be restoring his own life as well. He devoted a great deal of attention to beautifying the mission, especially the gardens. For the adobe mission church, he would eventually bring in a new reredos from Spain.

By the time that Father O'Sullivan arrived, the old ruined mission had started to attract a small tourist trade. Tourists and impressionist landscape painters were attracted to its colorful gardens and the captivatingly tragic ruins of the Great Stone Church—not to mention the hospitable welcome that they received from Father O'Sullivan. Among the artists who came were Franz Bischoff, Alson Clark, Colin Campbell Cooper, Fannie Duval, William Wendt, and others from the artists' colony that then existed in Laguna Beach. Both Charles Percy Austin and the Belgian portrait artist Joseph Kleitsch resided for a time at Mission San Juan Capistrano. Kleitsch painted Father O'Sullivan's portrait, and Austin illustrated a small book that the pastor wrote about the mission in 1912.

Father O'Sullivan also utilized interest in the mission's population of swallows as a means of eliciting outside interest in the mission. The little swallows had been at the mission since the day that Father Serra first set foot on the site, but they would not be identified as the signature icon of the mission until the second decade of the twentieth century. A 1915 article in the *Overland Monthly* magazine had observed that cliff swallows (*Petrochelidon pyrrhonota*), which range seasonally across most of the temperate Western Hemisphere, return annually to summer at Mission San Juan Capistrano, dwelling in small, cone-shaped nests that they construct of mud on the sides of buildings.

Ornithologists have recently determined that the swallows from San Juan Capistrano winter in Corrientes Province in Argentina and fly 7,500 miles between there and California twice a year. Flying as high as 2,000 feet to take advantage of favorable air currents, they make the commute in about a month. They typically arrive at the mission each year around the feast day of St. Joseph's Day, which falls on March 19. As the story of this phenomenon spread in the early twentieth century, a growing number of tourists and birdwatchers began coming each year to observe the swallows' return.

The mission also became a magnet for Hollywood celebrities in the early days of the silent screen. Many came to visit, and in January 1911, superstar Mary Pickford married Irish screen idol Owen Moore at Mission San Juan Capistrano. The marriage would last just nine years, but Mission San Juan Capistrano was about to enjoy a renaissance that would elevate it to national prominence.

After the painters came the writers. In 1919, when the author Johnston McCulley created a character named "Zorro" for a series of adventure stories, he chose Mission San Juan Capistrano as the setting for the first story about Zorro's exploits. Numerous books as well as films and television programs using the fictional hero would be set in California's mission period of the early nineteenth century.

In 1930, Father O'Sullivan collaborated with author Charles Saunders in a compilation of stories about the mission and town of San Juan Capistrano that was entitled *Capistrano Nights*. Father O'Sullivan's contribution was his version of the tale of the iconic birds, *The Legend of the Swallows' Return*. His story told of a missionary who observed townspeople brushing swallow nests off buildings, and who then invited the swallows to

make their homes at the mission—where all were welcome. So popular were the little birds during the early twentieth century that NBC Radio made a live, nationwide broadcast of the swallows' return in 1939.

Even after Father O'Sullivan's death in 1933, the mission grew more and more popular. After the artists and authors came the songwriters, or at least one man in particular who put San Juan Capistrano in the charts. Leon Rene would pen his legendary, romantic number-one hit song "When the Swallows Come Back to Capistrano." It would enjoy a thirteen-week run on the Hit Parade in 1940, and would be covered by artists from Glenn Miller to the Ink Spots. Today, naturally, it is the official song of the city of San Juan Capistrano.

When the swallows are out of town, Mission San Juan Capistrano attracts visitors to a variety of music and cultural events that it hosts throughout the year. These range from its annual Christmas tree lighting in December to the Music Under the Stars and the Capistrano Valley Symphony series.

Since suffering damage in the 1987 Whittier Earthquake, the mission has embarked on a massive restoration project. While Father Serra's church and most of the quadrangle have been stabilized, the Great Stone Church was placed on the list of 100 Most Endangered Historical Sites by the World Monuments Watch program in 2002.

CHAPTER EIGHT

MISSION SANTA CLARA DE ASÍS

THE STRATEGIC PLAN FOR THE San Francisco Bay Area developed by Viceroy Antonio Bucareli called for a settlement near the Golden Gate, the mouth of the bay, and another settlement near the foot of the bay. Father Junípero Serra, meanwhile, planned missions for both locations. The first requirement would be satisfied by the founding of Mission San Francisco de Asís in 1776, the latter by the creation of Mission Santa Clara de Asís a year later.

For the southern mission, Father Francisco Palóu had identified a site on San Francisquito Creek near present-day Palo Alto in 1774. However, when Captain Juan Bautista de Anza and Lieutenant José Joaquin Moraga had made their overland trek from Monterey to the Golden Gate in June 1776, they identified another location farther south, near the river that they named Rio de Nuestra Señora de Guadalupe, or Our Lady of Guadalupe. In November, Father Tomas de la Peña surveyed this location and concurred that it would

be a better place. On January 5, 1777, Father Peña and Lieutenant Moraga returned to the Guadalupe River. One week later, on January 12, Father Peña installed a cross and said Mass in a temporary structure. The second San Francisco Bay Area mission, and the eighth in the Alta California mission system, was founded.

As had been predetermined earlier in the master plan for the Alta California missions, this mission would be named Mission Santa Clara de Asís for St. Clare of Assisi, the cofounder, with St. Francis, of the Order of Poor Ladies, and first abbess of San Damiano. Born in Assisi in July 1194, she was the devout daughter of the wealthy Favorino family, inspired by the teaching of St. Francis to change her privileged life to one of poverty and good works. In 1212, she became his follower, and together they formed the Order of Poor Ladies, also to be known as the "Poor Clares." She took up residence with the Benedictine nuns of San Paolo, near Bastia, and was soon joined by her younger sister

Above: Built in 1825, the long-standing Santa Clara mission church featured trompe l'oeil, or false perspective, renderings of pillars and statues on its facade.
Opposite: When the church was rebuilt following the 1926 fire, it was decided to render the former false perspective details on the facade in three dimensions.

Agnes, or in Spanish, Inés. Later canonized as St. Agnes of Assisi, Clare's sister would be the namesake of Mission Santa Inés. St. Francis established a convent for the Poor Ladies near the chapel of San Damiano, which became the permanent home of

the order. In 1228, Clare successfully resisted attempts by Pope Gregory IX to compel her to renounce the Franciscan vow of poverty for her order. In 1234, when San Damiano was attacked, Clare took a ciborium from the chapel, went to the window,

and held up the Blessed Sacrament in the view of the invaders. A dazzling light is said to have then caused the enemy to retreat. Clare passed away on August 11, 1253, after a long illness and was canonized by Pope Alexander IV in 1255.

Two weeks after the first Mass at the seventh mission, Father José Murguía arrived at Mission Santa Clara de Asís from Monterey. With him were Spanish troops leading a pack train of supplies and cattle to form the basis for the mission farms. Over the coming months, the missionaries worked to construct their buildings and to make contact with the native Muwekma people. A branch of the Ohlone, the Muwekma are related to the Yelamu Ohlone people who lived in what is now San Francisco. They are both part of the group that anthropologists now refer to as Costanoan. As was the case with most native Californians, they were hunter-gatherers, hunting small game and gathering acorns from the oak trees that were then plentiful in the Santa Clara Valley. They also fished the bay and surrounding streams.

As had been the case at Mission San Francisco de Asís, the Ohlone living near Mission Santa Clara de Asís would eventually accept the Franciscan missionaries into their midst. However, at Santa Clara de Asís, records show that there were incidents that led to friction in the early years. A few of the Ohlone stooped to thievery, and the Spanish soldiers turned to

violent punishment when the perpetrators were caught. Eventually, the missionaries were able to mediate the problems and get on with the business of baptizing neophytes.

The forces of nature would turn out to be a greater adversary than the native people. Two years after the mission was founded, disaster struck. As had been the case with Mission San Antonio de Padua, the missionaries had sited Mission Santa Clara de Asís in a flood plain. High water would be a problem each winter, but in January 1779, the Guadalupe River jumped its banks completely, and the two years of work on the mission infrastructure was swept violently downstream.

A temporary wooden church was constructed, and was dedicated by Father Junípero Serra on November 11, 1799. Meanwhile, Father Murguía searched for a permanent location on higher ground. On February 19, 1781, the cornerstone was laid for a new adobe church that was designed by Father Murguía himself. He is said to have worked extremely hard on the construction project. Indeed, he would work himself to death. On May 11, 1784, just four days before Father Serra arrived from Carmel for the formal dedication, Father Murguía passed away. The dedication of the first adobe church at Mission Santa Clara de Asís took place, to the peals of ringing mission bells, on May 16. Father Serra was on hand, as were both Father Peña and Father Palóu. The following day, Father Serra

Contact Information:
MISSION SANTA CLARA DE ASÍS
Santa Clara University
500 El Camino Reál
Santa Clara, CA 95053

Mission office: (408) 554-4023

Web site:
www.scu.edu/visitors/mission

officiated at the first Mass said in "Father Murguía's Church."

The Great Earthquake of December 8, 1812, that did so much damage in Southern California, and which destroyed the Great Stone Church at Mission San Juan Capistrano, was felt as far north as San Francisco. At Mission Santa Clara de Asís, the damage was sufficient that Father Magin de Catala and Father José Viader undertook plans for yet another mission church. It would not be the last. The fourth church at Mission Santa Clara de Asís was completed in 1819, and the fifth was dedicated in 1825. It would stand on the site of the present mission church for 101 years.

Meanwhile, the location of "Father Murguía's Church" would be forgotten, and it would remain so until 1911, when the cornerstone that he had laid in 1781 was discovered during a construction project. The fourth church, in turn, would become a residence for neophyte boys in 1825 and serve as such until 1836.

As would be the case throughout most of the Alta California mission chain, Mission Santa Clara de Asís would prosper during the early nineteenth century. Through the end of 1832, a total of 8,536 baptisms and 2,498 weddings had been performed at the mission. These numbers were the highest of any of the twenty-one missions in Alta California.

The fields and pastures of Mission Santa Clara de Asís also flourished, even after Mexico declared its independence from Spain in 1821. Six years later, there were still 14,500 head of cattle and 15,500 sheep at Santa Clara de Asís. However, the loss of Spanish government support and Mexico's general disinterest in the mission chain would begin to take its toll. By 1832, Santa Clara de Asís's herd of cattle was down to 10,000 and the sheep now numbered 9,500 head.

The following year, the Secularization Act was passed and the Alta California mission system began to collapse. Most of the missions were secularized in 1834, but Mission Santa Clara de Asís would not find itself in that condition until December 27, 1836. The mission church made the transition to a parish church serving the nearby cities of Santa Clara and San José, and the Franciscans remained in charge. The mission church would be kept up, but the other structures around what had

Above: A series of remodelings undertaken under Jesuit auspices between 1861 and 1887 dramatically changed the look of the Santa Clara mission church. Wood framing designed to simulate stone encased the old adobe, and two matching wooden towers were built.
Below: This retouched photo of the October 1926 fire shows the wooden facade and towers as they were about to disappear forever.
Opposite: The mission grounds form the heart of Santa Clara University.

been the mission quadrangle collapsed from disuse and misuse.

For more than a decade after secularization, the Santa Clara Valley surrounding the Mission Santa Clara de Asís church was a quiet place of villages and haciendas. Farther north, near Mission San Francisco, the town of Yerba Buena became the city of San Francisco, but remained a sleepy fishing village. The catalyst that would change all of this was the January 1848 discovery of gold in the Sierra Nevada. With the gold rush of 1849, the population of the entire San Francisco Bay Area mushroomed.

In 1850, the same year that California became a state, the archdiocese of San Francisco chose to transfer the church at the former Mission Santa Clara de Asís from one Catholic religious order to another. From the Franciscans, the church went to the Society of Jesus—the Jesuits. It was an interesting turn of events to have a Franciscan institution transferred to the Jesuits eighty-three years after all of the missions in Baja California had been transferred from the Jesuits to the Franciscans. An important part of the activities of the Jesuit Order is higher education, and the Jesuits envisioned the former mission as the centerpiece for their first college in the state of California.

Bishop Joseph Alemany formally appointed Jesuit priest Father John Nobili as pastor of the Santa Clara mission church on March 4, 1851. Nobili arrived to assume his post on March 19, and two months later Santa Clara College, the first college in California, officially began classes. For its first two years, however, these classes were strictly college preparatory. College-level classes at the school would not be added to the curriculum until 1853, and most of the students would be at the high school level until late in the nineteenth century.

The mission church grew in importance as the centerpiece of Santa Clara College. When he became president of the college in 1861, Jesuit Father Burchard Villiger began the first of a series of remodeling projects at the church and the surviving Mission Santa Clara de Asís buildings. The emphasis was on a facelift for the crumbling church. As was the case farther south at Mission San Luis Obispo de Tolosa, a wooden facade and a wooden campanario were constructed to update the look of the old adobe church. A quarter-century later, under college president Father Robert Kenna, further remodeling was aimed at increasing the capacity of the church and constructing a pair of towers.

In 1912, the college officially became the University of Santa Clara, with the addition of a school of engineering and a school of law. A business school would be added in 1926. The college preparatory high school component would be detached from the university in 1925, becoming the Bellarmine College Preparatory in 1928.

The first major natural disaster to strike Mission Santa Clara de Asís had been water in 1779. The second, 147 years later, would be fire. At 7:00 a.m. on the morning of October 24, 1926, an electrical fire that started in the north tower of the church ignited a blaze that engulfed the entire structure. Though the building was completely destroyed, many of the historical objects and artwork from inside were saved.

During the nineteenth century, the focus of mission remodeling had been on modernization. By the third decade of the twentieth century, there was a growing nostalgia for the original look and feel of the historic missions, and the paradigm had shifted to historic restoration. With this in mind, the Jesuits at the University of Santa Clara decided to rebuild their church not as it had existed before the fire, but in an approximation of the appearance of the 1825 church. The new plan involved going back to the single-tower design, but the footprint of the church was kept larger than the 1825 church because the increased seating capacity was necessary.

One of the most interesting features of the new church was on the facade. It was known from nineteenth-century photographs that the flat front of the 1825 church had been painted with a trompe l'oeil false perspective depiction of pillars, arches, and statues. In the new version, it was decided to render all of this in three

Above: The rose garden adjacent to the mission church on the campus of Santa Clara University.
Opposite: This old adobe wall is the only surviving intact remnant of the Mission Santa Clara de Asís quadrangle. The olive trees near the wall date back to 1825. An adjacent building that once housed stables, storerooms, and workrooms was remodeled as the Santa Clara University's Adobe Lodge, a faculty and senior staff club that also contains a modern kitchen and a banquet room.

dimensions. Inside the church, paintings and carvings were done to reproduce the look and feel of the earlier church. The present mission church was formally dedicated May 13, 1928.

Originally an all-male institution, the University of Santa Clara became coeducational in 1961 and became Santa Clara University in 1985. While it remains as the official chapel for the 8,000 students attending school at the 104-acre university campus, the mission church is open to the public for Masses, as well as for baptisms, funerals, and weddings.

CHAPTER NINE

MISSION SAN BUENAVENTURA

During the later part of the eighteenth century, the area of the California coast on the Santa Barbara Channel opposite the Channel Islands was home to an especially large number of villages occupied by Chumash people. It was in this area that the Franciscans had planned to establish the third mission after anchoring the chain with Mission San Diego de Alcalá in the south and Mission San Carlos Borromeo de Carmelo in the north.

However, while he was in the north, Father Junípero Serra chose to establish the third just south of Mission San Carlos Borromeo de Carmelo, and Mission San Antonio de Padua thus came third. After that, other factors, including the political urgency of the San Francisco Bay Area missions, would intervene to delay the intended "third" mission for about a dozen years. By the time that the missionaries arrived at this location opposite the Channel Islands, eight other missions had been created throughout Alta California.

The missionaries and Spanish soldiers would finally arrive in March 1782, having come overland from Mission San Gabriel Arcángel. In this expedition, Father Junípero Serra and Father Pedro Benito Cambón were accompanied by Governor Felipe de Neve. On Easter Sunday, March 31, Father Serra said Mass near the shoreline of the Santa Barbara Channel, at a place that the Chumash called Miscanaga, and formally dedicated Mission San Buenaventura. He named the mission for St. Bonaventure, the cardinal of Albano, whom the Franciscan Order has always regarded as one of its leading scholars. Among his students were Matthew of Aquasparta and John Peckham, who later became archbishop of Canterbury. Born near Viterbo in 1221, Bonaventure died at Lyon, France, in July 1274.

According to legend, Bonaventure was cured of a nearly fatal illness as a child in a miracle performed by St. Francis of Assisi. He joined the Franciscans at some point between

Above: The south side of the mission church at San Buenaventura as it appeared in 1936, two decades before the church was remodeled. Among other changes, the 1957 restoration reduced the size of the windows to approximate their appearance in 1809.
Opposite: The area around the main altar as it appears today.

1238 and 1243 and became a lecturer at the University of Paris in 1248. In October 1267, St. Bonaventure and St. Thomas Aquinas received their doctorates on the same day. In 1260, the Franciscan Order commissioned Bonaventure to write a biography of St. Francis. Published three years later, it would become recognized as the definitive work on the man. In 1271, Bonaventure was considered as a possible successor to Pope Clement IV, but instead of himself, he successfully promoted Theobald Visconti of

Piacenza, who took the name of Gregory X. The following year, Bonaventure initiated the steps that would lead to the canonization of France's King Louis IX, who is coincidently the namesake of Alta California's eighteenth mission.

In 1273, Bonaventure humbly but unsuccessfully resisted Pope Gregory's effort to make him cardinal of Albano. As the story goes, when the papal emissaries found Bonaventure washing dishes outside a convent near Florence, he told them to hang the cardinal's mitre in a tree until he had finished his task. In his new role, he served as the pope's right-hand man at the Ecumenical Council in Lyon in 1274. Bonaventure passed away during the conference and was extensively eulogized.

Bonaventure was so well liked during his lifetime that there was an almost immediate groundswell for canonization after he died. Indeed, Dante Alighieri had placed him as one of the saints in the Paradise volume of his *Divine Comedy*—and this was *before* Bonaventure had passed on. His actual canonization would occur in 1482. His many published works— including commentaries on Plato and Aristotle as well as on the Gospels— would be widely read and discussed, and many would regard him as one of the preeminent philosophers of the Middle Ages. It has been said that while St. Thomas Aquinas enlightened the mind, St. Bonaventure inflamed the heart.

Father Serra departed Mission San Buenaventura shortly after the dedication, leaving Father Cambón in charge. This would be the last mission that would be established in Father Serra's lifetime.

Father Cambón would complete the first mission church within two years, and he had soon introduced an extensive agricultural operation. Utilizing the labor of Chumash neophytes, he oversaw the construction of an elaborate water system that spanned the seven miles between the mission and the Ventura River.

During his extensive survey voyage on the west coast of North America between 1792 and 1794, the great English explorer Captain George Vancouver visited Mission San Buenaventura twice. In his journals, he extolled Father Cambón's gardens as being among the most splendid he had ever observed. Among the wide variety of fruits and vegetables grown here by the Franciscans were bananas and figs. Captain Vancouver recalled that he had been pleased to have been able to procure fresh produce from the Franciscans.

The original mission church at San Buenaventura burned down in about 1794, and work was begun that year on a more permanent stone church. This building was under construction for much longer than any comparable mission church in Alta California. It was finally dedicated on September 9, 1809, with the first Mass celebrated on the following day. The

Above: Details of the decorative work within the mission church includes depictions of the Crucifixion (left) and of Our Lady of Guadalupe (right). The figure to the left of the crucifix is Our Lady of Sorrows, a depiction of Mary in the sorrow that she experienced at Jesus' Crucifixion.

reredos, said to have been carved in the sixteenth century, was brought in from the Philippines.

Three years and three months later, the Great Earthquake of December 8, 1812, slammed the region. The Great Stone Church at Mission San Juan Capistrano, then just six years old, was a total loss. Amazingly, a second earthquake, also with a magnitude of about 7.0 on the Richter scale, struck the Santa Barbara Channel area less than two weeks later!

The December 21 earthquake severely damaged the Mission San Buenaventura stone church, which, like

that of San Juan Capistrano, was virtually brand new. The campanario collapsed, but the main part of the church was still standing. This second quake in less than a fortnight was accompanied by a tsunami that is said to have been every bit as frightening to the residents of Mission San Buenaventura as had been the earthquake. Though the mission was located some distance from the high tide line of the ocean beach, it was barely above sea level and thus exposed to abnormally high waves. Reportedly, people were so nervous about further tidal waves that the mission was abandoned by its residents, who spent the winter in the higher

Above: Now on display at the mission museum, the wooden bells at San Buenaventura are said to have been the only ones used anywhere in the Alta California mission system.

Right: The top bell in the San Buenaventura campanario was installed during the 1950s with an automatic angelus device. The others are rung by hand. All of these bells are cast in bronze.

Contact Information:
MISSION SAN BUENAVENTURA
211 East Main Street
Ventura, CA 93001-2691
Phone: (805) 643-4318
Fax: (805) 643-7831

Web site:
www.sanbuenaventuramission.org
E-mail: mission@
sanbuenaventuramission.org
Gift Shop E-mail: giftshop@
sanbuenaventuramission.org

ground of the coastal hills. Though the repair work would take a year or more, the church at Mission San Buenaventura would eventually be mended, with buttresses added to protect it from future quakes.

Apparently, the trauma of December 1812 had few long-term effects on the prosperity of the mission. The neophytes returned to work the lush, cultivated fields, and to learn trades and study at the mission. The Chumash neophyte population would reach a peak of 1,328 just four years later in 1816. A yardstick of the level of activity at any mission is the number of baptisms and weddings that occur. Through the end of 1832, a total of 3,875 baptisms and 1,097 weddings had been performed at Mission San Buenaventura, which is about average, given the number of years that the mission was in operation.

Though relations with the local Chumash people are generally recalled as having been good, an incident with another tribe marked the low point in the history of the mission's interaction with the native people of Alta California. In May 1819, a group of Mojave people from the inland desert country near the Colorado River came to the coast to trade. There was an altercation between the Mojave and Chumash, in which Spanish soldiers intervened to jail several Mojave overnight. The following day there was a more serious fight between the troops and the Mojave, in which ten of the latter and two soldiers were

killed. Though there would be no further trouble at Mission San Buenaventura over this incident, it resulted in long-term animosity between the Spanish and the Mojave people elsewhere in Alta California.

The coastal missions were often visited by ships sailing the Pacific Ocean. As noted earlier, explorers such as George Vancouver stopped to procure supplies and pay their respects. However, not all the mariners from across the horizon came peacefully. In the autumn of 1818, the notorious French buccaneer Hippolyte de Bouchard was creating mayhem on the coast of Alta California. He would ransack Mission San Juan Capistrano and raid Monterey—where he failed to go inland to find and sack Mission San Carlos Borromeo de Carmelo. He also got into a fight with Spanish troops near Santa Barbara, but didn't attack the mission. In November, Bouchard's pirate ships were observed in the Santa Barbara Channel near Mission San Buenaventura. Father José Señan ordered the church vestments and valuables to be hidden in a cave, and he evacuated the people from the mission into the hills. They remained away from the mission for several weeks until they were sure that Bouchard would not return.

When Mexico declared its independence from Spain in 1821, the Spanish support for the missions evaporated and they were compelled to rely on self-sufficiency. This would continue for a dozen years until the

Above: The nave of the Mission San Buenaventura church, looking from the altar. Note the intricately painted beams in the ceiling. Opposite: A view of the church looking across East Main Street from near the fountain. Until the freeway from Los Angeles was completed to Ventura in 1969, Highway 101 ran on this street. Before that, it was the original El Camino Reál.

passage of the Secularization Act, by which the missions were each stripped of the land necessary for self-sufficiency. Most of the missions would be secularized by the end of 1834, but Mission San Buenaventura held out for another two years until June 1836. Rafael Gonzales, the unusually competent civilian administrator of the property, ensured a smooth transition, and the mission church went on to function as a parish church for several years.

Eventually, the former mission lands were rented to Don José Arnaz and Narciso Botello. In 1845, the notorious Pío Pico, Alta California's last Mexican governor, began selling the mission churches themselves. The one at San Buenaventura went to Arnaz, and the proceeds went in Pico's pocket. Nevertheless, the church seems to have continued to be used as such even after it technically became private property. A man named Henry Miller visited here in 1856 and met the French priest who was in residence at that time. Miller reported that the orchard was in "fine condition" and shared a bottle of wine made at San Buenaventura. He noted that it was "excellent but was very strong."

The title to the mission church building and some of the adjoining property was finally returned to the Catholic Church in May 1862. In the meantime, the clay tile roof had been damaged in a moderate earthquake in January 1857 and had been replaced by a wood shingled roof. This was probably done under the stewardship of the same French priest who had met with Miller a year earlier. By now, the city of Ventura was growing up around the mission. Officially incorporated in 1866, Ventura received a major influx of settlers from the eastern United States in the years after the Civil War. One such man was Thomas R. Bard, who came west to manage the property that was owned by the legendary nineteenth-century railroad baron Tom Scott. Bard put down roots in Ventura County and became one of the first to make his fortune in the California oil boom. He later served as the first president of the Union Oil Company. As the early missionaries had discovered, the coastal country near Ventura is ideal for growing fruits and vegetables, and this allowed the city and the county to prosper. Early in the twentieth century, Ventura became an important citrus region, and indeed, it was growers here who formed Sunkist, the world's largest citrus production organization.

Between 1878 and 1895, Father Cyprion Robio served as pastor at Mission San Buenaventura. Many of the missions were saved from deteriorating into ruins during the late nine-teenth century, but they suffered quite an opposite fate. In order to make them useful as parish churches, they were modernized. Such was the case of San Buenaventura under the well-meaning Father Robio. Among his updating projects were enlarging the windows and installing stained glass. Also added was a fresh coat of paint. Unfortunately, this went over the top of mural work that had been done by the Chumash neophytes a century before. In the late 1880s, several buildings around the quadrangle were torn down. So too was the original sacristy, which was removed to make way for a school—which was not built until 1921. Clearly, the school was important, and the stained glass windows made for a nice ambience, but the remodeling was not in keeping with the original 1782 look of the building.

It was during the 1920s that many of the additional buildings adjacent to the church were added. After the school, there was a section to provide living quarters for the nuns, and by 1929 a new sacristy and a museum were in place. In 1957, a new round of remodeling was completed at the church itself. Undertaken by Father Aubrey O'Reilly, this effort was to undo many of the changes made in the 1880s and 1890s, and to restore the church to a closer approximation of the original structure. The windows were returned to their original size, and in 1976, the wood shingle roof was replaced with a new one with old-fashioned clay tiles.

Above: The statue of the Madonna in the mission garden. Opposite: A view of the nave at Mission San Buenaventura looking toward the altar. The use of the red carpeting supercedes the original rough clay tile floor.

CHAPTER TEN
MISSION SANTA BÁRBARA

K NOWN TODAY AS THE "Queen of Missions," Mission Santa Bárbara is the only one of the twenty-one missions to have had a continuous Franciscan presence from the day it was founded until the present time. Ironically, it is a mission that Father Junípero Serra was actually *forbidden* from establishing.

As had been the case with Mission San Diego, Mission Santa Bárbara would derive its name from one that had been assigned to the location in 1602 by Sebastián Vizcaíno. It was on December 4, the feast day of St. Bárbara, that he sailed through what is now the Santa Barbara Channel, and anchored near the present-day site of the city of Santa Barbara. The location was also well known to Gaspar de Portolá and to Father Junípero Serra, but locations other than Santa Barbara were higher on the list of priorities for settlements and missions.

On April 21, 1782, just three weeks after the dedication of Mission San Buenaventura, the Spanish estab-

lished the Presidio of Santa Bárbara in the heart of what is now the city of the same name. With Lieutenant José Francisco de Ortega in command, it was the fourth and last presidio, or military post, established by the Spanish in Alta California after San Diego, Monterey, and San Francisco. It was also the only presidio to be established without a mission being founded at more or less the same time. Father Junípero Serra, who had been at San Buenaventura for the dedication there, made the forty-mile journey to the new Presidio of Santa Bárbara, said Mass at the facility, planted a cross, and made preparations for the intended mission.

However, Governor Felipe de Neve, who had been present for the Mission San Buenaventura dedication, vetoed Father Serra's plan. He told the Franciscans that there were enough missions and that he wanted no more to be established while he was governor. As the story goes, the governor was displeased with the growing economic and political power that was

Above: The west tower and tiled roofs, as viewed from the quadrangle, in the late afternoon.
Opposite: Mission Santa Bárbara has a dramatic setting beneath the Santa Ynez Mountains.

being wielded by the Franciscans in Alta California. Apparently, he felt his temporal authority being undermined, and the controversy between the king of Spain and the Jesuits over the Baja California missions just fifteen years earlier was still fresh in his mind.

Though Neve was superseded as governor later in 1782 by Pedro Fages, the notion of a tenth mission remained in bureaucratic limbo. Coincidentally, both Neve and Father Serra passed away in 1784. Some sources say that Father Serra had

Above: A quiet corner at Mission Santa Bárbara. The rich artistic heritage of the mission is not only in what is on the walls, but the walls themselves.

gotten word of the new governor's approval for Mission Santa Bárbara just before he died. In any case, Fages had finally approved the tenth Alta California mission, and it would be nice to think that both Neve and Father Serra had gotten the word.

Father Serra's successor, Father Fermín Lasuén, selected a site in the hills overlooking the Presidio of Santa Bárbara that the native Chumash people called Taynayan. Past experience in San Diego, San Francisco, and Monterey had shown that the presidios were selected on the basis of their strategic position in relation to the harbor. Missions needed to be located farther inland, where there was more abundant water and more land that could be made agriculturally viable. The missionaries also liked to keep the Spanish military posts at arm's length.

On December 4, 1786, the feast day of St. Bárbara, Father Lasuén formally dedicated Mission Santa Bárbara. A second dedication twelve days later was attended by Governor Fages. The mission's namesake was a legendary virgin martyr who is said to have lived in the fourth century. She is widely mentioned in Christian texts dating back to the seventh century. The daughter of a wealthy pagan named Dioscorus, she was murdered by him for converting to Christianity. A pious man named Valentinus buried the bodies of Bárbara and another martyr named Juliana, and their grave site became a place where

pilgrims prayed for solace and healing. According to the story, Dioscorus was struck dead by lightning, and for this reason St. Bárbara is invoked in prayers for protection against fires and explosions. She is also the patron saint of artillerymen.

Father Lasuén named Father Antonio Paterna as senior missionary, and he set about making contact with the local people. As would be the case at the other missions along this section of the coast, the Chumash people welcomed the missionaries and were reportedly eager to become converts to Christianity. In fact, many of the Chumash leaders, including a chief named Yanonali, were baptized at Mission Santa Bárbara. Through the end of 1832, a total of 5,556 baptisms had been performed at the mission. Mission Santa Bárbara had more baptisms than any other mission in Southern California except Mission San Gabriel Arcángel. Through 1823, there would be 1,486 weddings performed at Mission Santa Bárbara, the third highest number south of the San Francisco Bay Area after San Diego and San Gabriel Arcángel. A large and orderly residential area for the Chumash neophytes was laid out immediately next to the northwest side of the mission quadrangle. At its peak, this large, rectangular village had more than twice the area of the quadrangle.

The Chumash, who had traditionally been hunter-gatherers, would now learn agriculture. In addition to fields of barley, beans, corn, and

Above: The afternoon sun filters through the windows at the old mission church. This a view of the nave from near the altar.

Contact Information:
**MISSION SANTA
BÁRBARA**
St. Barbara Parish
2201 Laguna Street
Santa Barbara, CA 93105

Parish office: (805) 682-4713
Fax: (805) 687-7841

Web site:
www.sbmission.org/home.html

wheat, the Franciscans and their neophytes planted orange and olive orchards and put in vineyards. The 4,500 tons of wheat that were grown at Mission Santa Bárbara through 1832 put it in fifth place among all the missions and in a dead heat with the 4,550 tons grown at Mission San Diego, where there was a seventeen-year head start. Among all other crops combined, Mission Santa Bárbara

ranked seventh with 3,053 tons. By 1832, the mission system of Alta California had clearly passed its golden age. At Mission Santa Bárbara, the livestock inventory illustrates this. It would drop from 5,200 head of cattle in 1806 to 1,800 in 1832, and from 11,221 head of sheep in 1803 to 3,200 in 1832.

In 1786, Father Paterna had also begun constructing the first wood and

adobe mission buildings. What was probably intended to be a permanent mission church was completed at the site in 1794. It would stand for eighteen years as additional structures were added and the mission quadrangle was completed.

In 1795, after suffering two years of drought, the Franciscans at Mission Santa Bárbara began planning for an aqueduct system to tap mountain

Above: A view of the arcade on the convento building west of the mission church. The Franciscans have had their offices in the convento on this site for over two centuries.

streams such as Pedregoso Creek to irrigate the mission's fields and orchards, and to serve the water needs of the people living at the mission. The largest of the reservoirs, which was completed in 1806, is still in use.

In December 1812, two earthquakes, each measuring about 7.0 on the Richter scale, struck southern Alta California in less than two weeks. The first decimated Mission San Juan Capistrano, while the second, on December 21, did considerable damage to both Mission San Buenaventura and Mission Santa Bárbara. As had been the case at San Juan Capistrano, the mission church at Mission Santa Bárbara was essentially destroyed. Unlike San Juan Capistrano, however, the church would be rebuilt. The new church would be twenty-seven feet wide and 161 feet long, standing forty-two feet high, with a facade that was patterned after a Roman building designed in 27 BC by Vitrivius. The cornerstone was laid in 1815, three years after the earthquake. The church, which still stands, was formally dedicated on September 10, 1820, with Governor Pablo Solá in attendance.

Like Mission San Carlos Borromeo de Carmelo and Mission San Buenaventura, the 1820 mission church at Santa Bárbara had a single tower flanking the entrance, but a second tower was added in 1831. The new tower collapsed the following year, but was replaced in 1833.

In 1821, just a year after the dedication of the new Mission Santa Bárbara church, Mexico declared its independence from Spain and the government subsidies to the mission system ended. A dozen years of decline would lead to the final blow of secularization. It was in 1833, the same year that Mexico passed the Secularization Act, that Alta California Governor José Figueroa decided to turn all of the missions north of Mission San Antonio de Padua over to Mexican-born Franciscan priests from the College of Guadalupe de Zacatecas. This included both Mission San Carlos Borromeo de Carmelo, the traditional headquarters of the mission system, and Mission San José, which was the residence of Father Narciso Durán, who was then serving as father-president. Against the backdrop of this sudden turn of events, Father Durán decided to relocate the Alta California mission system headquarters to Mission Santa Bárbara in 1833. A year later, when the Secularization Act was ratified, the mission system essentially ceased to exist.

Mission Santa Bárbara would fare better than most missions after secularization. Most of the missions would become parish churches, and in many cases the priests would continue to be of the Franciscan Order for a while. At Mission Santa Bárbara, the Franciscans would remain. At most missions, a civilian administrator was appointed by the Mexican governor. At Mission Santa Bárbara, the job went to a Franciscan—Father Durán.

Father Durán was later joined by Father Francisco Garcia Diego y Moreño, a Zacatecan Franciscan who had been appointed as the first bishop of California.

When both Father Durán and the bishop died in 1846, Pío Pico, Alta California's last Mexican governor, initiated plans to seize and sell Mission Santa Bárbara. Shortly thereafter, California became part of the United States. The American government was predisposed to recognizing church ownership of the missions, and the title to Mission Santa Bárbara was finally granted back to the Franciscans in 1865. Throughout the two intervening decades, however, the Franciscans had remained in residence at the mission.

The Franciscans continued to expand their presence at Mission Santa Bárbara, and between 1868 and 1877 they operated a high school and junior college at the mission complex. In 1896, a seminary for training priests, called the School of Theology for the Franciscan Province of St. Barbara, was started. Now known as the Franciscan School of Theology, the seminary was relocated to Berkeley, California, in the summer of 1968.

While many missions decayed, and a few became parish churches, Mission Santa Bárbara continued to prosper as a center of Franciscan activities in the West. The prominence of Mission Santa Bárbara is illustrated by the number of important dignitaries who went out of their

Above: The famous fountain at Mission Santa Bárbara was installed in 1808. It was designed to receive water from the aqueduct system uphill from here, and to supply water to the lavandería, which was downhill to the right.

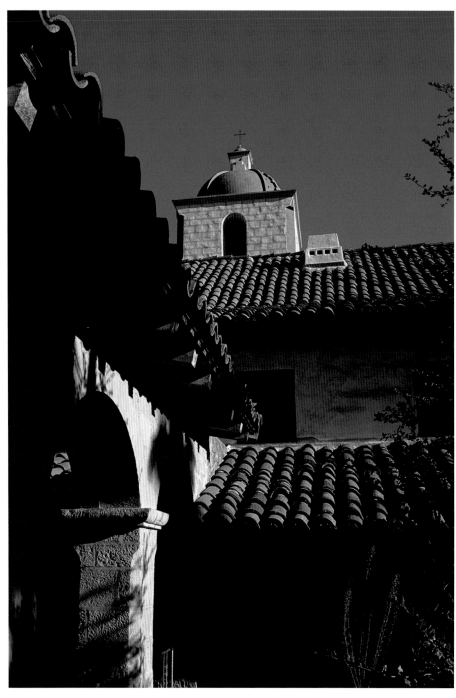

Above: One of the twin towers of the mission church as seen inside the quadrangle. First used on the missions in the late eighteenth century, the red clay tiles have come to define the mission architectural style widely replicated across California today.
Opposite: A dramatic view of the main altar at Mission Santa Bárbara.

way to travel to the California coast to see the mission. At Christmastime in 1882, the Queen of Missions received a visit from the daughter of Britain's Queen Victoria. Princess Louise is said to have been the first woman to be shown the gardens within the cloistered quadrangle at Mission Santa Bárbara. A century later, in 1983, Victoria's great-great-granddaughter, Queen Elizabeth II, paid a royal visit to Mission Santa Bárbara.

The mission also received three presidential visits over the span of a dozen years. Benjamin Harrison visited in 1891 with little fanfare, but William McKinley took part in a parade when he came to Santa Barbara in 1901.

Two years later, Father Ludger Glauber entertained President Theodore Roosevelt, who came calling during the same California trip on which he made his famous visit to Yosemite Valley in the company of John Muir. Roosevelt reportedly complimented the Franciscans on their having saved a large number of eighteenth and early nineteenth-century Chumash artifacts in their museum.

The early decades of the twentieth century would see a great deal of restoration work being done at the missions throughout California. However, much of what would be done at Mission Santa Bárbara was in response to the June 29, 1925, earthquake, which measured 6.8 on the Richter scale. Brick and masonry buildings throughout the city of Santa Barbara suffered considerably, and State Street, the main thoroughfare, was filled with rubble. Up on the hill, Mission Santa Bárbara suffered damage to both the church and the monastery. Los Angeles architect Ross Montgomery would supervise the two-year reconstruction project, which involved replacing the unreinforced masonry walls dating back to 1820 with steel-reinforced concrete. The effort throughout this restoration was to maintain the original appearance of the church and other structures. Unfortunately, this would not be the end of the story. In 1950, cracks began to appear in the work done in the restoration. This required that the facade be removed and rebuilt. Later in the decade, additional construction would be done, altering the west wing and adding a second quadrangle, which had been planned as early as 1796.

Today, the Franciscan Province of St. Bárbara has its headquarters in Oakland, California. Franciscans from this province live and serve in places that cross ethnic, cultural, and economic boundaries throughout California, as well as in seven other states and around the world. They continue to minister among the American Indian people of the Southwest. Though their headquarters is no longer here, the province maintains a retreat center at Mission Santa Bárbara. The mission church is now the centerpiece of the Franciscan Parish of St. Bárbara.

CHAPTER ELEVEN
MISSION LA PURÍSIMA CONCEPCIÓN

WHILE MANY CALIFORNIA missions are located in urban areas and are today confined to the few buildings surrounding the mission church, the La Purísima site contains 966 acres that are part of the original mission lands. As such, a visit to La Purísima gives us an unparalleled sense of the scale of the original missions. After having laid in ruins for a century, the site was excavated by archaeologists and rebuilt in the 1930s. The renovations resulted in it being the most completely restored of all the California missions.

The eleventh of the missions, La Purísima was founded on December 8, 1787, on the south side of the Santa Ynez River, then known as the Santa Rosa River, near the present town of Lompoc. The location was four miles southwest of the present mission site. Father Fermín Lasuén said the celebratory Mass on that day, dedicating the new mission as La Purísima Concepción de María Santísima, or the Mission of the Immaculate Conception of Mary Most Pure.

It had been a year since Mission Santa Bárbara was founded, and the idea was to situate the mission roughly halfway between Santa Bárbara and San Luis Obispo. It was a wet winter and little work was done toward constructing the mission buildings until March of 1788, after the rainy season had passed.

A month after the construction crews arrived from Santa Bárbara, the first resident priests, Father Vicente Fuster and Father José Arroita, arrived to take charge of the mission and to begin ministering to the Chumash people of the area. By 1798, there were 920 people living at the mission, including craftsmen and soldiers, as well as clergy and Chumash.

During those years, a temporary mission church and many additional buildings were constructed on the original site. Within a few months of La Purísima being founded, the surrounding fields were cleared, and bar-

Above: The altar within the mission church at La Purísima Concepción.
Opposite: The exterior of the mission church, with the pink campanario in the foreground.

ley, beans, corn, peas, and wheat were planted. The priests also brought in root stock so that orchards and vineyards could be established. These plantings included, of course, the olive trees that were common to all the missions.

Livestock, including goats, horses, mules, pigs, and sheep, were brought in. With the wool from the sheep, weaving became an important activity at La Purísima. To serve this farmland, an elaborate water system was constructed to divert water from

the streams that flowed from the coastal hills. Initially, the outside supplies came overland from the missions to the south, but gradually the mission became self-sufficient in most things. Occasionally, however, ships would arrive with manufactured goods imported from Spain or Mexico, especially porcelain, textiles, and metal items.

The permanent mission church at La Purísima was completed in 1802, and two years later, Father Mariano Payeras arrived to take charge of the mission and to begin his nineteen-year term as senior missionary. By this time, La Purísima was at its peak in terms of its population, with nearly 1,600 people living there, including around 1,522 Chumash neophytes. It was also in 1804 that Mission Santa Inés was established about twenty miles east of La Purísima near the town of Solvang.

The mission's livestock herds were reported to have numbered about 20,000 at the beginning of the nineteenth century, meaning that La Purísima had also become an economic force to be reckoned with. Products that were sold or bartered included cattle and horses, as well as leather goods, wool, soap, and candles. Bartering provided goods from other missions and settlements, while the sale of certain goods provided the hard currency that was necessary to pay the craftsmen who lived and worked at the mission for varying periods of time.

Above: Mission La Purísima Concepción is unique in that its setting is little changed since the eighteenth century. This view is looking east from the carpenteria toward the corrals and the neophyte dormitory.
Left: The ruins of the mission church as photographed by Henry F. Withey for the Historic American Buildings Survey in May 1937 during the restoration project.
The Civilian Conservation Corps had undertaken the daunting task of rebuilding the mission complex with original methods and materials in 1934. Roof tiles were made with clay that they dug from the surrounding hillsides. The three main buildings were completed by December 1941, when La Purísima Concepción was dedicated as a State Historical Monument.

Above: This aqueduct was part of the original water system that was built to serve the needs of the mission complex at La Purísima Concepción. The mission church is visible in the distance.
Right: The restored colonnade at the priests' residence building.

Contact Information:
LA PURÍSIMA MISSION STATE HISTORIC PARK
2295 Purísima Road
Lompoc, CA 93436
Phone: (805) 733-3713
Fax: (805) 733-2497

Mission Web site:
www.lapurisimamission.org

California State Parks Web site:
www.parks.ca.gov

E-mail:
lapurmis@sbceo.org

The early years of the nineteenth century would mark a golden age for Mission La Purísima, although there would be times of difficulty. A series of smallpox outbreaks spanning the four years ending in 1807 wiped out nearly a third of the Chumash living at La Purísima, a tragedy that left no family untouched.

As it was with most of the Southern California missions, the defining natural disaster in the history of Mission La Purísima was the pair of magnitude 7.0 earthquakes that devastated so much of the Spanish infrastructure throughout the region in December 1812.

Centered in the Santa Barbara Channel area just to the south, the second of these struck on December 21, just two weeks after La Purísima celebrated its twenty-fifth anniversary. The initial temblor did a great deal of damage to the mission church at La Purísima, but the first aftershock thirty minutes later left it, along with most of the mission's buildings, in a pile of rubble. To make matters worse, the December rains turned into a deluge and floods destroyed much of what had survived the earthquake.

Despite this tragedy, the people of La Purísima rebounded and rose to the challenge. Father Payeras decided to rebuild the mission buildings on higher ground, and chose a site in a little valley north of the river, about four miles northeast of the original location. This site was officially dedicated on April 23, 1813.

The new Mission La Purísima that took shape at this location was to be a much larger complex than the original. The construction methods also changed. Just as modern California building codes are constantly being revised to take seismic concerns into consideration, the seismic standards that the builders at La Purísima took into account were much more stringent in 1813 than they had been in 1802. To make the new structure more earthquake-resistant, the builders used stone to reinforce the adobe, and the

Above: The courtyard located behind the shops and quarters contained many of the facilities that were necessary for the daily needs of the mission residents. The beehive-shaped horno (oven) was used for baking bread and tortillas.
Opposite: The soldiers' sleeping area in the cuartel, which was located at the end of the shops and quarters nearest the church.

walls of the mission church were built more than four feet thick.

There were other architectural changes in the new mission that would make La Purísima unique. This time, instead of laying out the complex as a quadrangle with the church at one corner, the buildings were constructed in a line. Beginning with the church at the western end of the complex, the buildings are in a line leading eastward and uphill, parallel with the valley, which was known as Los Berros for the watercress that grew along the small seasonal stream that flowed there.

Further up the valley were the fields and orchards and an irrigation system with a series of dams and reservoirs. These would be linked to the buildings at the mouth of the valley by a system of aqueducts that still exists. While similar elaborate engineering projects were completed at other missions, the extent of the work has been lost as cities and towns have grown up around the missions. At both La Purísima and Mission San Antonio de Padua the grounds remain, but only at La Purísima are we still able to see the fields and aqueducts more or less as they were when the mission was active.

Much of the work on these water projects was probably in response to the severe drought of 1816 and 1817, during which crops failed and large numbers of livestock perished. Despite such setbacks, La Purísima generally flourished during this period. Meanwhile, Father Payeras was growing in prominence within the mission establishment. In 1815, he was named to a four-year term as father-president of the Alta California mission system. During this time, he would choose to remain at La Purísima, rather than relocating to Carmel. This made La Purísima the de facto capital of the California missions during that period. In 1819, Father Payeras was also named to head the Franciscan Order in California, a post the hardworking friar held until he passed away on April 28, 1823.

The following year, the generally harmonious relations between the Spanish and the Chumash in central California began to unravel. An incident on February 21, 1824, at Mission Santa Inés involving the mistreatment of a Chumash neophyte from La Purísima Concepción led to a widespread revolt in which people were killed on both sides. The revolt spread to Mission Santa Bárbara as well as to La Purísima, where the rebel Chumash seized control of the mission. The governor responded by sending a contingent of troops down from the Presidio of Monterey to retake La Purísima by force.

After a three-hour battle, Father Rodríguez, the senior missionary at La Purísima Concepción, negotiated a

Chumash surrender. However, the conflict had cost the lives of sixteen Chumash and one soldier. Subsequently, seven of the leaders of the revolt were executed and eighteen others were sent to prison. The latter was an effort by the authorities to send a message to other would-be rebels.

Meanwhile, Mexico had declared its independence from Spain in 1821 and it was widely understood that the Mexican government intended to secularize the missions. The missions had been subsidized by the generosity of the Spanish monarchy, and Mexico was anxious to not take over this responsibility. Through the end of 1832, a total of 3,522 baptisms and 1,029 weddings had been performed at the mission.

When the Secularization Act was ratified in 1834 and Mexican governor José Figueroa issued the long-awaited secularization order, the mission system collapsed. The Franciscans soon abandoned many of the missions. The clergy at La Purísima left to consolidate their activities with the church at Mission Santa Inés. Approximately 200 Chumash neophytes would stay on at La Purísima for the next decade, continuing to farm the land. In 1845, the land was sold to a former Spanish don from Los Angeles named Juan Temple for a reported $1,100 (the equivalent of about twenty times that amount in today's dollars).

For nearly a century, the land remained essentially untouched. Stone and other building materials were

Above: The pottery building and the kiln were located behind the building that housed the priests' quarters and their chapel.
Opposite: This reconstructed oxcart is typical of those that routinely traveled El Camino Reál at the beginning of the nineteenth century.
Behind are La Purísima Concepción's shops and quarters (left) and priests' quarters (right).

undertook the project in 1934. The reconstruction involved rebuilding the structures on their original foundations using early nineteenth-century construction methods and tools.

Adobe bricks were manufactured on site, and roof tiles were fired in handmade kilns using local clay. The hardware that was used in the restoration was made at La Purísima by blacksmiths working with period equipment.

By December 1941, when La Purísima was dedicated as a state park, work had been completed on the three largest structures, the mission church, the priests' quarters, and the large building that housed the barracks and workshops. A second phase of restoration began in 1951, in which restoration of ten buildings containing thirty-two rooms was completed. It has been described as the most comprehensive restoration project involving a California mission.

Today, the park is managed by the Department of Parks and Recreation in cooperation with a volunteer organization known as the Prelado de los Tesoros de la Purísima, or Keepers of the Treasures of La Purísima. Together they present a wide variety of year-round interpretive programs for visitors. California fourth-graders and visitors from around the world come to this once-remote corner of the California coast to enjoy these programs, or simply to visit the mission buildings and walk the grounds.

taken from the buildings for other uses, and they collapsed into ruin. In 1903 the area was part of an acquisition by the Union Oil Company, which held the land for three decades without drilling for oil on the property. Meanwhile, the Catholic Church, which had officially held the title to the site of the old church since 1874,

donated the church ruins to Santa Barbara County.

In 1933, recognizing the archaeological significance of La Purísima, Union Oil donated what it owned of the former mission acreage to the state. The California Division of Beaches and Parks, the predecessor to today's Department of Parks and

Recreation, purchased some additional parcels and acquired the mission church from the county.

Having acquired La Purísima, the state invited the federal government to restore La Purísima. Under the direction of the United States National Park Service, the newly formed Civilian Conservation Corps

CHAPTER TWELVE

MISSION SANTA CRUZ

WHEN IT WAS FOUNDED BY Father Fermín Lasuén on August 29, 1791, Mission Santa Cruz seemed to have everything going for it. There was plenty of water and potential farmland nearby, and it overlooked Monterey Bay. Indeed, the lights of Monterey were visible at night across the bay. The native Ohlone people knew this place on which the twelfth mission would be located as Aulintac, but the Franciscans would call it Misión la Exaltación de la Santa Cruz, or the Mission of the Exaltation of the Holy Cross. Actually, that name dated back to October 17, 1769, when Gaspar de Portolá had camped here on banks of the San Lorenzo River, erected a cross, and named it for the Holy Cross.

The Holy Cross, or True Cross, is the one on which Jesus Christ was executed. It is probably the most venerated relic in Catholicism, and the most holy and enduring of all Christian symbols. The exact location of the True Cross—if any fragments still exist—cannot be verified.

However, there are numerous reports of fragments having been found, and of them existing at various locations. For example, legend holds that the True Cross was located in AD 326 by Helena, the mother of the Roman emperor Constantine, during her pilgrimage to Jerusalem. She is said to have put a fragment in a silver reliquary that was later purloined by the Persian king Chosroes, but rescued in 628 by Emperor Heraclius II. Another popular story tells that in 569, Radegunda, queen of the Franks, acquired another fragment from Emperor Justinian II. She then hosted a solemn feast and founded a monastery at Poitiers, France, in its honor. Many similar legends exist, but there are no stories of such a fragment ever having been brought to Alta California.

At the mission on Monterey Bay named for the Holy Cross, the infrastructure progressed quickly. The first wooden church had been built on the flood plain of the San Lorenzo River in the heart of what is now downtown

Above: The peaceful garden behind the little church at Mission Santa Cruz. Opposite: A tall cypress and the campanario tower over the mission church.

Santa Cruz, but this mistake was soon rectified by a move up a nearby hill— now known as Mission Hill—to the present location. The first building completed on Mission Hill in 1792 was the convento, which was a long, narrow building 176 feet long and

more than fifteen feet wide. When this adobe structure was damaged by a rainstorm in 1796, it was replaced by a wooden building 193 feet long.

The cornerstone of the adobe mission church was laid on February 27, 1793, and it was dedicated on May

rebuilt in 1824 and augmented by additional ones in 1833.

In 1794, the same year that the church was completed, a two-story granary was built behind the church's sacristy and music room as an extension of the building. The quadrangle is said to have been completed in 1795. Based on measurements recorded in 1835, the quadrangle measured 250 by 238 feet. The assorted mission workshops that were noted to have been part of the quadrangle included rooms for weaving, wool carding, and spinning, as well as a blacksmith shop, a leather shop for shoes and saddles, and a hatmaker's shop. Outside the quadrangle were the soapworks, candle factory, and meat processing area. The orchards were to the north of the quadrangle and the cemetery was to the east.

In the meantime, history records that relations between the mission and the native population were not as good as those between the Ohlone at the missions on San Francisco Bay. Late in 1793, the animosity boiled over. On the night of December 14, a group of people from Quiroste, a village in the mountains near Point Año Nuevo, about twenty-five miles north of Santa Cruz, attacked the mission. Several structures were burned and several people were injured, but no fatalities were recorded. According to contemporary accounts, the catalyst for the attack seems to have been a dispute between an Ohlone woman who had

become a Christian and an Ohlone man who had not. Early in 1794, Spanish soldiers from the presidios at San Francisco and Monterey, aided by Ohlone people loyal to the mission, hunted down the eight alleged leaders of the attack and sent them to prison in San Diego, never to return.

In terms of the total number of baptisms and weddings performed, Mission Santa Cruz was about average for a mission established in the 1790s. Between 1791 and the end of 1832, a total of 2,439 baptisms and 827 weddings would be performed at the mission.

Despite the 1793 incident, the mission's relations with their Spanish neighbors would create more difficulties for Mission Santa Cruz than their relations with the Ohlone. In 1797, a settlement known as the Branciforte Pueblo was established across the river from the mission. This planned community had been named for, and authorized by, the Sicilian-born Miguel de la Grua Talamanca, who held the title Marques de Branciforte. As of 1794, Talamanca had also held the title of Viceroy of New Spain. As such, he reigned over all of Spain's possessions from Central America to Alta California. He was just as unpopular in Mexico City as the Branciforte Pueblo would be unpopular at Mission Santa Cruz. While he was recalled to Europe in 1798 after just four years, the pueblo would be a thorn in the side of the Franciscans—and the Ohlone as well—for two decades.

10 of the following year. Available data indicates that the permanent adobe church was 113 feet long, twenty-nine feet wide, and twenty-six feet tall. Its interior dimensions are thought to have been 103 feet by twenty-seven feet. It had a choir loft at the rear with a stairway on the west. In 1811, the facade was replaced and a tile roof added. Three buttresses were added to the south and east sides of the church in 1813, and these were

Above: Neophyte quarters that were part of the Mission Santa Cruz quadrangle are preserved at the Santa Cruz Mission State Historic Park. Completed in about 1824, they are among the best preserved of the neophyte residences at any of the missions. The campanario of the mission church can be seen in the background in the center, while the steeple of Holy Cross Church is visible on the right. Opposite: The replica church. Its inscription, "O Crux Ave Spes Unica," translates to "Hail O Cross, the Only Hope."

Contact Information:
MISSION SANTA CRUZ
Holy Cross Church
126 High Street
Santa Cruz, CA 95060
Phone: (831) 423-4182
Fax: (831) 423-1043
Holy Cross Church Web site:
www.holycrosssantacruz.com

Santa Cruz Mission
State Historic Park
144 School Street
Santa Cruz, CA 95060
Phone: (831) 429-2850
California State Parks Web site:
www.parks.ca.gov

The Branciforte Pueblo was planned as an ambitious upscale housing development, but it turned into what was essentially a base for smugglers. With its saloons, dance halls, and other houses of ill repute, it created an environment that was diametrically opposite to what the missionaries were trying to do. Theft of mission property and assaults on neophytes became an epidemic. At one point, a group of thieves from Branciforte robbed Mission Santa Cruz when the priests were across the mountains attending an event at Mission Santa Clara. In another incident, a priest was allegedly murdered in his sleep.

In 1818, when the notorious privateer Hippolyte de Bouchard sailed to California to plunder, the missionaries and neophytes headed toward Mission Nuestra Señora de la Soledad for safety. Bouchard raided Monterey, but ignored Santa Cruz and turned south. However, while the mission's occupants were away, the men of Branciforte went up the hill to Mission Santa Cruz and helped themselves to food, tools, and other supplies. As Bouchard was doing at that moment at Mission San Juan Capistrano, the Branciforte men raided the Franciscans' wine cellar and drank their fill. They would later explain that they were simply protecting the mission property from the pirates.

The notion of closing Mission Santa Cruz was seriously considered

but rejected. Though the mission remained, it would never fulfill the promise of a rosy future that seemed almost within Father Lasuén's grasp on that sunny August day in 1791. Though the total baptisms were about average, the population of Mission Santa Cruz peaked at just 523, making it the smallest of all the missions.

One of the first missions to be secularized in 1834, Mission Santa Cruz soon fell into disrepair. It was not, however, completely abandoned as a church. Though the campanario collapsed in 1840, the church continued to be used. Father José Antonio Suárez del Reál would remain in residence until he returned to Mexico in 1845. After that, other priests visited from time to time to bring the sacraments to the neophytes and other Catholics in the Santa Cruz area. Father Anzar commuted in from Mission San Juan Bautista occasionally. Father Francisco Lebaria said Mass at Mission Santa Cruz occasionally in 1851, and Father Sebastián Filoteo was in residence in 1853. Father Juan Comellas was at Mission Santa Cruz between 1854 and 1856, and was succeeded by Father Benito de Capdevilla. The story of the old mission church finally came to its sad conclusion when it was turned to rubble in the earthquake that occurred on February 16, 1857.

Meanwhile, the city of Santa Cruz had grown up all around the old mission site, and Holy Cross Parish had replaced Mission Santa Cruz as the Catholic parish for the city. In 1857, not long after the earthquake, the parish began construction of a wood-frame church and a new rectory near the ruins of the old mission. This church was thirty-six feet wide, 110 feet long, and it stood twenty-seven feet high. In 1861, work began on a parish girls' school. Opened in 1862, it accommodated 200 students, who were taught by the nuns of the Daughters of Charity of St. Vincent de Paul.

In the meantime, Father Capdevilla passed away in 1861, and Father Angelo Casanova came across the bay from Monterey to serve as pastor of Holy Cross Parish until 1868. It was during his tenure that a pair of bell towers were added to Holy Cross Church. The next pastor, Father Joaquin Adam, introduced such modern innovations as gas lighting for the church. He also built a side altar, imported a large Spanish crucifix, and started a boys' school at Holy Cross Parish.

Father Hugh McNamee, who became pastor in 1883, decided to build an all-new brick church on the site of the original mission church. Demolition of the existing structures began in 1885, and the cornerstone of the new church was laid on July 4, 1886. The bell was cast in San Francisco by Weed and Kingwell, using two cracked bells taken from the old mission. Father McNamee would have other surviving mission bells recast in 1901. Construction of the new church, whose appearance was described by such terms as

"English-Gothic" and "Protestant," was complete by 1889. It was 138 feet long and fifty-seven feet wide, making it the largest structure to have occupied the site. As such, it extended into the area of the original mission cemetery. The church was formally dedicated on September 15, 1889, with Bishop Francis Mora present.

After the brick church was completed, the 1862 wood-frame church was torn down. A granite archway was erected at the church and dedicated by Holy Cross Parish on September 25, 1891, to commemorate the centennial of long-gone Mission Santa Cruz.

During the 1920s, as the notion of mission restoration was sweeping California, plans were laid to construct a full-size replica of the old Mission Santa Cruz church. Such a strategy was promoted by many in the parish who were sorry to have seen it torn down in the first place, and by Father O'Reilly, who had taken over as pastor in 1918. Complete accuracy would have required placing the replica on the original site, but because the 1889 Holy Cross Church was now at this location, an alternate site about a block away was selected. San Francisco architect H. A. Minton, who had designed the Bank of America building on Montgomery Street in San Francisco, was hired for the project and a fund-raising campaign was begun.

As the story goes, the stock market crash of 1929 washed away the money earmarked for this project

Above: The peaceful nave of the Mission Santa Cruz church bathed in the golden light of a cool winter afternoon.
Opposite: The church and tower at the replica Mission Santa Cruz. With no details to supply scale, one can easily imagine the original church, which had been twice this size. The tower fell in 1840 after forty-six years, and the church collapsed in 1857.

like the San Lorenzo River washed away the church at the original mission site. Against this backdrop, a reconstruction effort did go forward, but the result would be a half-scale replica of the original church that was designed by the architectural firm of Ryland, Estey and McPhetres, and funded in large part by Gladys Sullivan Doyle. The cornerstone was laid on February 14, 1932. The replica still stands. Other parts of the original mission quadrangle about a block away were restored by the State of California and are open for viewing

today as Santa Cruz Mission State Historic Park.

A half-century later, the bad luck that had plagued Mission Santa Cruz in its early days suddenly returned. During the 1980s, the interior of the Holy Cross Church was extensively remodeled in preparation for its 1989 centennial. On October 17, 1989, 220 years to the day after Gaspar de Portolá first set foot at Santa Cruz, the magnitude 7.1 Loma Prieta Earthquake struck northern California. Centered in the mountains just above Santa Cruz, it hit this coastal commu-

nity especially hard. The entire downtown was heavily damaged. On Mission Hill, the replica Mission Santa Cruz church survived, but Holy Cross Church, just reconsecrated after a hundred years, was rendered unusable. Services were moved to the parish hall, but on June 30, 1990, the parish hall burned to the ground.

The repair and reconstruction work would take a decade, but by the end of the twentieth century, Holy Cross Church was completely retrofitted and a new parish hall had been constructed.

CHAPTER THIRTEEN
MISSION NUESTRA SEÑORA DE LA SOLEDAD

Тне story of Mission Nuestra Señora de la Soledad opens with a scene worthy of a classic novel. The year was 1769. Father Juan Crespí was making his way north with the expedition headed by Gaspar de Portolá. Following the slow-moving Salinas River, the Spaniards were traveling north toward Monterey Bay through the broad valley that lies across the Santa Lucia Mountains from the Pacific Ocean. No Spanish explorers were known to have ever come this way before, so it was entirely uncharted territory. The weather was hot, and the valley appeared empty and desolate.

Portolá, Father Crespí, and the others camped for the night by the river, thinking that they were alone. They were sure that there were no other people for as far as the eye could see, but they were wrong. As they set up camp, they were approached by several of the Esselen people who made this broad valley their home. Neither side knew the other's language, but in the course of other's language, but in the course of

the conversation, Father Crespí thought he heard one of the men use the Spanish word *soledad*. Father Crespí was probably projecting, because the word was likely on his mind. It means solitude or loneliness, and it seemed to describe what the Spanish perceived as a very lonely place.

As the story goes, Father Junípero Serra passed this way two years later and spoke with some of the Esselen people. To his surprise, he heard a woman say that her name was Soledad. As had been the case with Father Crespí in 1769, it was probably another word, but the coincidence amazed Father Serra because the name seemed to summarize the spirit of the Salinas Valley in 1771.

In fact, the place already had a name. According to Pedro Font, who studied the Esselen, the place was called Chuttusgelis. The people who lived here were the Eslenahan branch of the Esselen, a very small subgroup of one of the least numerous tribes in Alta California. Alfred Kroeber, in

Above: The ruins of the 1832 chapel as they appeared in 1918. The corner on the left was all that remained when the reconstruction project began in 1954.
Opposite: The interior of the reconstructed chapel. The figure at the center is a depiction of Nuestra Señora de la Soledad, or Our Lady of Solitude. She is dressed in black.

his 1925 *Handbook of the Indians of California,* estimated that the Esselen numbered between 500 and 1,000 at the time that the Spanish arrived. Sherbourne Cook later calculated an

estimate of about 1,300 based on the assumption that the people occupied an area of about 625 square miles with a population density of 2.1 people for each square mile. This territory

included all of the area west of the Salinas River as far as the Pacific Ocean and as far north as Carmel Valley where Mission San Carlos Borromeo de Carmelo was located. The Eslenahan branch were a mere handful of Esselen people who lived near the place that the Spanish now called Soledad.

Gradually the valley of the Salinas River—then known as Rio de Monterey—would become less lonely. The route that had been taken by the early explorers would become the well-traveled El Camino Reál. Other missions were established along the route at San Luis Obispo de Tolosa and San Antonio de Padua, but Chuttusgelis was just a waypoint. Finally, in 1791, two decades after Father Serra first passed this way, Father Fermín Lasuén decided to establish a mission, the thirteenth in the chain, in this valley. He dedicated

it as Mission Nuestra Señora de la Soledad, or Our Lady of Solitude. The name refers to Mary, the mother of Jesus Christ, as she is depicted after the Crucifixion, experiencing the loneliness and sorrow of her loss. She is also called Nuestra Señora de las Angustia, or Our Lady of Anguish, and Nuestra Señora de los Dolores, meaning Our Lady of Sorrows. Devotion to Nuestra Señora de la Soledad was especially common in Spain in prayers said on Holy Saturday, the day before Easter. This tradition in Spain is traced to Queen Juana mourning the loss of her husband, King Philip I, in 1506.

Mission Nuestra Señora de la Soledad was formally established by Father Lasuén on October 9, 1791, and work on a temporary church at the site began at once. The church was completed in 1792, but the mission was not off to an easy start.

Above: A surviving segment of the old quadrangle wall. Most of it had collapsed during the nineteenth century.
Right: The foundation lines of the original Nuestra Señora de la Soledad mission church, which stood from 1797 and 1831.
Opposite top: The reconstruction of the 1832 chapel, as restored in 1954–1955.
Opposite bottom: The Nuestra Señora de la Soledad mission complex as it appeared in about 1870 when it was being used as a farmstead. The 1832 chapel and the convento were still standing at this time.

Contact Information:
MISSION NUESTRA SEÑORA DE LA SOLEDAD
36641 Fort Romie Road
Soledad, CA 93960
Phone: (831) 678-2586

neophyte population peak at 688 in 1805, then decline by 13 percent over the next five years.

When he passed away on November 26, 1818, Father Ibañez became the first and only Franciscan to be buried at Mission Nuestra Señora de la Soledad. However, four years earlier, the governor of Alta California, José Joaquin de Arrillaga, had died at the mission while on an inspection tour along El Camino Reál. He had asked to be buried at the mission in a Franciscan robe, and he was.

Whereas drought had plagued Nuestra Señora de la Soledad in its early years, flooding would curse the years after the death of Father Ibañez. The flood of 1824 would destroy the mission church, and the smaller chapel that was built to replace it was washed away by floodwaters in 1828.

Rebuilding was not an easy process. Reports made by the missionaries complained about a shortage of trees that could be harvested for lumber of a decent size.

The flood of 1832 would essentially mark the end of the mission. A storehouse was converted for use as a chapel, but no effort was made to continue to expand or undertake any major building work. The Secularization Act passed the Mexican congress the following year.

The last of the Franciscans at Mission Nuestra Señora de la Soledad was Father Vicente Francisco de Sarría, who had previously founded Mission San Rafael Arcángel in 1817, and who

Drought conditions prevailed in the area through most of the decade. Nevertheless, work proceeded on a larger mission church, which was completed in 1797, and extensive irrigation work was done to utilize the water in the Salinas River to serve the mission's fields.

Today, the valley is an important agricultural region, but for Mission Nuestra Señora de la Soledad, farming was not easy. Between 1791 and 1832, the mission produced crops totaling

3,420 tons, including 2,065 tons of wheat. This placed it seventeenth among the twenty-one missions.

An inventory of mission property that was compiled in 1827 listed Mission Nuestra Señora de la Soledad as having 5,400 sheep on three ranchos, two of which were shared with Mission San Carlos Borromeo de Carmelo. Nuestra Señora de la Soledad also had 4,000 head of cattle and 800 horses in 1827. An inventory done in 1836 after secularization listed

3,246 head of cattle, 2,400 sheep, and thirty-two horses.

Despite the best efforts of the Franciscans, the lonely place remained true to its name. Thanks to drought and disease, none of the Franciscan fathers posted here remained for long. Finally, the revolving door stopped when Father Florencio Ibañez arrived here in 1803. He would remain until his death 1818, serving longer at Mission Nuestra Señora de la Soledad than any other priest. He watched the had served as father-president of the mission system in 1823 and 1824. Father Sarría collapsed and died while saying Mass at Mission Nuestra Señora de la Soledad in May 1835. He was not buried at the mission, but was carried by neophytes to Mission San Antonio de Padua for burial. Mission Nuestra Señora de la Soledad has had no resident priest since.

Through the end of 1832, a total of 2,131 baptisms and 648 weddings had been performed at the mission. These were the lowest numbers of any of the eighteen missions that were founded prior to 1804. In his study of the Esselen people, Sherbourne Cook estimated that 951 Esselen people were baptized at the missions. Probably all of these baptisms would have taken place at either Mission Nuestra Señora de la Soledad or at Mission San Carlos Borromeo de Carmelo. Among the most unusual baptisms performed at Nuestra Señora de la Soledad was that of a twenty-year-old Nootka man in 1794. The Nootka people live on the northern part of Vancouver Island in what is now British Columbia. There is no mention of how he came to be in the Salinas Valley, unless he had somehow traveled south with Captain George Vancouver, who visited Alta California around this time.

Being in a less desirable location than many other missions, the property was not sold until 1845, more than a decade after secularization. The buyer was a man named Feliciano Soberanes,

Above: A group of people explore the tumbled-down ruins of the priests' wing of the convento in 1902.
Opposite: The priests' wing of the convento was restored in 1963 and it is now used as a museum and gift shop.

who probably used it for grazing. The following year, when Governor Pío Pico began selling off the mission churches themselves, there was little of value, other than a few roof tiles, at Mission Nuestra Señora de la Soledad. When the United States government formally restored the missions to the Catholic Church, many of them contained still functioning or operable churches, but at Nuestra Señora de la Soledad, so little remained that it was left vacant.

It was not until after World War II that any effort would be made to try to restore any buildings at the deserted site. In 1954, the Native Daughters of the Golden West began work on the small chapel. It was restored and was dedicated on October 9, 1955, the 164th anniversary of Father Fermín Lasuén's dedication of Mission Nuestra Señora de la Soledad. Eight years later, a reconstruction of the missionary residence was completed and opened to the

public. The foundation of the mission church that was destroyed in the 1824 flood, along with the graves of Father Ibañez and Governor Arrillaga, have been located, but no reconstruction of the church has been planned.

Today, the mission chapel is part of the Catholic Parish of Soledad, but Mass is held at the chapel only on special occasions. Two annual fund-raising events, the June Barbecue and the Fall Fiesta, are held to provide money for upkeep.

CHAPTER FOURTEEN

MISSION SAN JOSÉ

AFTER THE ESTABLISHMENT OF two missions in 1791, six years would pass before the Franciscans would add to the mission chain. It was the biggest time lag that had yet been experienced in the program. At issue, as it often is, was the cost. As discussed in the following entry on Mission San Juan Bautista, Father Fermín Lasuén developed an argument for additional missions along El Camino Reál that ultimately persuaded Viceroy Miguel de la Grua Talamanca, the Marques de Branciforte, to lift the suspension so that four missions could be founded in 1797. The first of these was not on El Camino Reál, but on the opposite side of San Francisco Bay from that highway. This one probably won approval because of Spain's strategic interest in staking its claim to the Bay Area.

In 1795, Father Antonio Danti had traveled east from Mission Santa Clara de Asís to survey possible sites on the east side of the bay. He located a place, known to the local Ohlone people as Oroysom, that was within the present-day city limits of Fremont and reported back to Father Lasuén. When the authorization came through, Father Lasuén himself returned to the site near Alameda Creek that had been surveyed by Father Danti. On Trinity Sunday, June 11, 1797, he said Mass and formally established Mission San José. The new mission was named for St. Joseph, who is mentioned in the Gospels of Matthew and Luke as being the husband of Mary, the mother of Jesus Christ.

Coincidentally, Father Lasuén had chosen the same name that José Joaquin Moraga had used for a settlement, or pueblo, that he had established two decades earlier at the foot of San Francisco Bay. This settlement, which would evolve into today's city of San José, California, was about fifteen miles from the mission, and was much closer to Mission Santa Clara de Asís.

Leaving Father Isidore Barcenilla and Father Augustin Marina in charge, Father Lasuén departed for San Juan Bautista. By the end of July, the two

Above: The old 1809 church at Mission San José as it appeared in about 1860. Opposite: The new mission church, reconstructed as a replica of the 1809 structure, was dedicated on June 11, 1985, the 188th anniversary of the founding of the mission.

Franciscans and the Spanish soldiers who had been posted to the mission had completed several temporary structures, and a herd of cattle had been brought over from Mission Santa Clara de Asís. The first wooden church at Mission San José was completed in 1798.

Father José Antonio Uría arrived at the mission in 1799 as an assistant to Father Barcenilla, and he took over entirely when Father Barcenilla retired in 1802. Three years later, Father Uría began work on a large adobe church for the mission. In 1806, a year into the construction project, two new

Above: The Mission San José complex as seen during the 1860s. Newer wood-frame buildings had been interspersed among the old mission structures since secularization. The October 1868 earthquake would wipe out most of these original buildings.
Below: The old convento as it appeared during the 1850s. By this time, it had been converted for use as a roadhouse and hotel. The road that passed this way was one of the main routes that was taken by prospectors headed for the gold fields in the Sierra Nevada.

Franciscan fathers arrived to take over Mission San José. Father Buenaventura Fortuni would remain for twenty years. Father Narciso Durán would be at the mission for nearly three decades.

Formally dedicated by Father-President Estévan Tápis on April 22, 1809, the adobe church at Mission San José was thirty feet wide and 135 feet long. It was completed with a thatched roof, which was soon replaced with clay tiles. Within two years, the church was surrounded by a quadrangle that included a monjerío, as well as by more than eighty two-room adobe buildings constructed to house the growing number of neophytes who were living at the mission. By 1825, as the neophyte population reached 1,800, the number of homes would nearly double.

Father Durán is recalled as having been a great lover of music, as well as being a skilled musician in his own right. There are records of concerts given at the mission that featured a thirty-piece orchestra with as many as twenty violins. He also devised a simplified system of musical notation that permitted him to teach songs to his neophyte choir more easily. His 156-leaf parchment choir book is preserved at the Bancroft Library on the campus of the University of California at Berkeley.

On two occasions, Mission San José would have the distinction of serving as the headquarters of the Alta California mission system. Between 1824 and 1827, and again between

Above: A year after the October 1868 earthquake destroyed the remnants of the old Mission San José complex, the wood-frame St. Joseph's Church would be erected on the site. A steeple would be added later. The cemetery in the foreground predated St. Joseph's, and it is still there today.

Contact Information:
MISSION SAN JOSÉ
43300 Mission Boulevard
P.O. Box 3314
Fremont, CA 94539
Phone: (510) 657-1797

1830 and 1833, Father Durán served two of his three terms as father-president. Because he remained based at Mission San José, the headquarters moved with him.

Gradually, Mission San José evolved into one of the most important and successful of the Alta California missions. Through the end of 1832, a total of 6,673 baptisms (some sources say 6,737) and 1,990 weddings had been performed at the mission. In those terms, which were certainly an important yardstick for the Franciscans, Mission San José was one of the most successful missions in Alta California. Both San Francisco de Asís and Santa Clara de Asís exceeded San José on both counts, but elsewhere in Alta California, only San Gabriel Arcángel exceeded San José in terms of baptisms.

These figures obscure the fact that the mission would have a great deal of trouble keeping the peace with the indigenous people of the region. It was on the east side of San Francisco Bay that the coastal tribes had traditionally interacted with tribes from the San Joaquin Valley. These people were much less accommodating toward the missionaries than were the coastal tribes. Essentially, the mission became embroiled in the traditional animosity between the Ohlone of the Bay Area and the Yokuts people from the San Joaquin Valley. This conflict, which boiled over in 1828 and 1829, centered on a man named Estanislao (Stanislaus).

Estanislao was a Yokuts man in his late twenties, one of a sizable number of Yokuts people who had come to Mission San José to join the community and become neophytes. Father Durán took a liking to Estanislao, who distinguished himself as a fast learner and a skilled manager. Eventually, Estanislao became the alcalde, or mayor, of the neophytes at Mission San José. In 1828, Estanislao and a number of fellow Yokuts, including a man from Mission Santa Clara de Asís named Cipriano, traveled into the San Joaquin Valley, possibly on a hunting trip. While on this excursion, they decided not to return to the missions. Eventually, they became part of a band estimated to number in excess of 500. This group consisted primarily of former neophytes who had chosen to abandon mission life.

Attacks on isolated Spanish settlements were attributed to this group that was being led by Estanislao, and troops were dispatched from the Presidio of San Francisco. A Spanish force under Sergeant Antonio Soto caught up with Estanislao in

Above: Old St. Joseph's as it appeared in 1937, with its New England–style steeple. The mission-era convento is in the foreground.
Below: The convento was the only surviving structure from the original mission when this picture was taken in 1934. The automobile club took some liberties with their sign. The city of Oakland, across the bay from San Francisco, was never on El Camino Reál.

November, but were badly defeated. Soto himself would die of his wounds. In March 1829, another command, led by José Antonio Sánchez, attacked Estanislao, but again the Spanish were defeated. Lieutenant Mariano Vallejo, at the Presidio of Monterey, gathered a much larger force and went after the Indians in May 1829. Sánchez, who was still in the field, got into a heated argument with Vallejo over which force had the proper jurisdiction to lead the final assault against Estanislao. This dispute was worked out and the attack went forward. The Indians were thoroughly defeated, but Estanislao escaped. He made his way back to Mission San José, where he begged Father Durán for forgiveness. The missionary interceded on behalf of the former alcalde and Estanislao was granted a pardon. He would spend the rest of his life at the mission. Today, Stanislaus County in the San Joaquin Valley is named for him.

In 1833, the Zacatecan Franciscans took over the northern missions, and Father Durán departed Mission San José for Mission Santa Bárbara to formally relocate the head-quarters of the mission system to Southern California. Succeeding him at Mission San José would be Father Gonzales Rubio, who would stay on at the mission after it was secularized in 1834. Two years later, Governor Juan Bautista Alvarado appointed José de Jesus Vallejo, the brother of Mariano Vallejo, as the civilian administrator of Mission San José. Vallejo proceeded

to pilfer food and other supplies from the mission, reducing the people who stayed on after secularization to near starvation. In 1840, when William Hartnell, Alvarado's inspector general of the missions, reported these abuses to the governor, Vallejo was forced to resign.

In May 1846, Governor Pío Pico sold the remaining mission property to his brother, Andres Pico. Soon after, California would undergo a series of dramatic changes. In 1846, the United States flag was raised over California, and in 1850 it became the thirty-first state. In the meantime, the discovery of gold in the Sierra Nevada in 1848 touched off the gold rush of 1849. The latter saw a massive migration into California from the eastern United States and elsewhere. For those forty-niners who arrived at

Above: The main entrance at the 1985 Mission San José church is used on formal occasions. Visitors usually enter on the side.
Top left: The fountain in the garden has always been a welcome sight on those hot summer days in Fremont.

Above: The main altar within the nave at Mission San José's 1985 church reconstruction.
Opposite: The mission cemetery has been in use for two centuries. This grave dates from the period when the 1809 church still stood.

the Port of San Francisco, the land route to the gold fields would run directly through the lands that had once been part of Mission San José and essentially right past the mission's front door. The mission would get a new lease on life as a waystation on the road from San Francisco to the gold country.

In December 1856, a decade after Pío Pico sold the mission, the United States Lands Commission formally restored twenty-eight acres—including the surviving buildings, the cemetery and the gardens—to the Catholic Church. As St. Joseph Parish, it would serve the Catholics of this growing corner of the San Francisco Bay Area. Indeed, the town that grew up around the old mission would be known as "Mission San José" until it was incorporated into the city of Fremont a century later in 1956.

Through the years of uncertainty both before and after secularization, the mission church slowly deteriorated, despite efforts by Father Rubio and others to stabilize it. On October 21, 1868, the issues of maintenance and restoration became moot. At 7:53 that morning, an earthquake estimated at about 7.0 on the Richter scale ruptured the Hayward Fault. Five people were killed, extensive damage occurred from Berkeley to Fremont, and the mission church at the former Mission San José was destroyed. The pastor, Father Federy, ordered that the rubble be cleared and a wood-frame church be constructed on the site.

This church would stand as the centerpiece of St. Joseph Parish for more than a century. In 1982, a plan was put into motion to reconstruct the old mission church at Mission San José. The wood structure that had stood for 114 years—nearly twice as long as the old adobe church—was disassembled and relocated across San Francisco Bay to the city of Burlingame. Over the next three years, the mission church was meticulously reconstructed using original tools and methods, including adobe bricks made in the same way as they had been formed during the first decade of the nineteenth century. The wooden structure was joined using rawhide straps rather than nails, which were unavailable during the construction of the 1809 building.

The original hammered-copper baptismal font was returned to the church and railings at the altar and choir were manufactured, using as a model a piece of the original that was in the mission museum. Both the crystal chandeliers and the reredos were reconstructed using old records. Three of the original mission bells that were salvaged from the rubble in 1868—and preserved in the wood-frame church—were rehung, and a fourth bell that had been given away was returned.

The new Mission San José church was dedicated on June 11, 1985, the 188th anniversary of the original founding of the mission by Father Fermín Lasuén.

CHAPTER FIFTEEN

MISSION SAN JUAN BAUTISTA

AFTER THE ESTABLISHMENT OF both Mission Santa Cruz and Mission Nuestra Señora de la Soledad in 1791, six years would pass before the Franciscans would add to the mission chain. The basic issue underlying the six-year suspension in the establishment of new missions, ordered by Viceroy Juan Vicente de Guemes Pacheco y Padilla, was cost. Even if a mission was self-sustaining—and many were not—there was the cost to the Spanish colonial government for maintaining a garrison of soldiers to protect them. Father Fermín Lasuén's counterargument was that additional missions could actually save money for the treasury. As it was, caravans traveling on El Camino Reál required military escorts, especially when they had to spend the night in the middle of nowhere.

Father Lasuén argued that, by filling in the open spaces along El Camino Reál, the additional missions could serve as rest stops where caravans could spend the night in relative safety. This was the point at which the concept of missions located a day's ride apart finally emerged.

In 1794, Miguel de la Grua Talamanca, the Marques de Branciforte, became viceroy of New Spain. Though he is recalled as having been a scoundrel for his palace intrigues in Mexico City, the viceroy responded to Father Lasuén's proposal with uncharacteristic foresight. When it was finally approved, Father Lasuén moved quickly, establishing an unprecedented four missions in 1797 and a fifth in 1798. The first of these would be Mission San José, the fourteenth mission in the chain, and the third San Francisco Bay Area mission. The fifteenth would be Mission San Juan Bautista, the first of the five additional missions whose locations were essentially chosen to fill in open spaces along El Camino Reál.

Known to the native Mitsun people as Opeloutchom, or Popeloutchom, the site selected for the fifteenth mission was on El Camino Reál roughly midway between Mission San Carlos

Above: The gardens at Mission San Juan Bautista.
Opposite: Completed in 1812, the mission church has an entrance with three arches, an architectural device that references the unique triple nave arrangement within.

Borromeo de Carmelo and Mission Santa Cruz, although it was farther inland than either of these two missions. Work on the buildings and other infrastructure at the site began in the spring of 1797 under the supervision of Spanish Corporal Juan Ballesteros several weeks before the mission was formally established.

Father-President Lasuén was on hand to formally establish Mission San Juan Bautista on June 24, 1797, just

Above: The main entrance to the Mission San Juan Bautista complex is through the convento arcade. The city's plaza is on the right.

thirteen days after he founded Mission San José. The day was also the feast day of San Juan Bautista, or St. John the Baptist, to whom Father Lasuén dedicated the mission. Discussed primarily in the Gospels of St. Luke and St. Matthew, St. John the Baptist was a preacher who baptized people in the Jordan River during the lifetime of Jesus Christ. He foretold the coming of Jesus, stating that "I indeed baptize you with water, but there shall come one mightier than I, the latch of whose sandals I am not worthy to loose. He shall baptize you with the Holy Spirit." When Jesus came from Galilee to the Jordan River, he asked to be baptized by John as the means by which he would be manifest to the world as the Savior.

The area chosen for Mission San Juan Bautista was home to the Mitsun, who were part of the group of peoples whom the Spanish referred to as "Los Costanos," or "the Coastal People" because they inhabited the Pacific coastal areas around Monterey Bay and farther north. The Ohlone of the San Francisco Bay Area were also part of the Costanoan group. As with other Costanoan people, the Mitsun were hunter-gatherers who hunted small game, fished coastal estuaries, and gathered acorns, which they ground into meal using stone mortars.

Because Opeloutchom was a crossroads of sorts for many different Costanoan tribes, the neophytes at Mission San Juan Bautista would eventually include not just the Mitsun people, but members of a dozen other Costanoan and Esselen groups.

The missionaries and the Spanish troops who were building Mission San Juan Bautista did not realize that the site they had chosen was virtually on top of Alta California's notorious San Andreas Fault. A series of earthquakes would plague this especially susceptible mission throughout its history. The first severe temblors would be recorded in 1798 and 1800. The latter, which destroyed the original adobe mission church on October 11, is estimated to have measured 5.5 on the Richter scale.

Ground was broken for a new church on the present location on June 13, 1803. As the story goes, a description of the ceremonial laying of the cornerstone was placed in a bottle and buried near the cornerstone. It is not known to have ever been recovered.

Five years later, in 1808, Father Felipe del Arroyo de la Cuesta arrived at Mission San Juan Bautista with the church still under construction. This energetic young Franciscan had the idea to modify the floor plan of the church in a unique way. All of the previous missions had just a single nave. It was Father Cuesta's idea to add narrower parallel naves to either side. This would greatly enlarge the capacity of the church, but the three-part design was more structurally sound than a single large room. Dedicated in June 1812, the resulting church would be 188 feet long and seventy-two wide, but no arch would have to span the full seventy-two feet. The internal walls

Above: The arcade at Mission San Juan Bautista has changed little in appearance for more than two centuries, although the presence of the San Andreas Fault practically underfoot has caused a crack or two to appear from time to time.

Contact Information:
MISSION SAN JUAN BAUTISTA
Second and Mariposa Street
P.O. Box 400
San Juan Bautista, CA 95045
Phone: (831) 623-2147
Fax: (831) 623-2433
San Juan Bautista
State Historic Park:
(831) 623-4526

California State Parks Web site:
www.parks.ca.gov

would help support the roof and make the building more earthquake-resistant.

It had been planned that the reredos behind the Mission San Juan Bautista altar would be created by artists brought in from Mexico, but Father de la Cuesta considered the cost of such artisans to be prohibitive. A half-dozen years after the completion of the church, the Franciscan crossed paths with a young sailor from Boston named Thomas Doak. Depending on which version of the story one wants to believe, Doak had either been stranded in Monterey or had jumped ship. In any case, he was a skilled artist, and he agreed to paint the Mission San Juan Bautista reredos in exchange for room and board. When he was finished, he stayed on

as one of the first Yankees to settle in Alta California.

Construction of the big church had begun against the backdrop of a robust community of Spanish and neophytes. It is said that the first neophyte baptism at Mission San Juan Bautista occurred just two weeks after the dedication in 1797. A short time later, the son of Corporal Ballesteros would be the first Spanish child baptized here. Through the end of 1832, a total of 4,106 baptisms and 1,003 weddings were performed at the mission. It is recalled that Father Cuesta commonly dipped into the European classics, bestowing such baptismal names as Plato and Cicero upon newborn Mitsun neophytes. The cultural tide, however, flowed both ways. As

was the case with men such as Father Buenaventura Sitjar at Mission San Antonio de Padua, Father Cuesta made an effort to learn and speak the local languages. He mastered a number of dialects and wrote an extensive study of the Mitsun language.

The same year that the church was completed, Father Cuesta was joined at Mission San Juan Bautista by Father Estévan Tápis, who just retired after serving as father-president of the Alta California mission system. Father Tápis was the first permanent father-president to have retired, as both Father Serra and Father Lasuén had remained in the post until they died. At the age of fifty-six, Father Tápis was still a relatively young man with a number of good years left in him. These would be put to use in an expansive music ministry at Mission San Juan Bautista. As Father Narciso Durán was doing at Mission San José, Father Tápis would create an innovative color-coded system of musical notation that would allow large numbers of neophytes to learn to sing. The Mission San Juan Bautista choir was soon renowned throughout the Alta California mission system. Father Tápis would remain at San Juan Bautista as its music director until his death in 1825 at the age of seventy-one. The music that he wrote for the neophytes was reportedly still being used several decades later.

An interesting footnote to the musical history of Mission San Juan

Bautista involves a hand-cranked organ that reportedly came to the mission from San Carlos Borromeo de Carmelo after it had been left there by English explorer Captain George Vancouver during a survey voyage to the west coast of North America between 1792 and 1794. Reportedly, the neophytes greatly enjoyed listening to the instrument. It is not known what happened to it. A similar instrument still at the mission is believed to date from a period later than the 1790s.

Despite the best efforts of Father Cuesta and Father Tápis to communicate with the neophytes through their native languages and through the universal language of music, their flock eventually decreased. As was the case at the other missions, the early days of Mission San Juan Bautista saw the largest neophyte population at the complex. Ironically, the church capable of holding a thousand people was completed after the mission population had declined from that figure. The neophyte population at Mission San Juan Bautista stood at about 500 at the turn of the century, more than doubled by 1805, but shrunk back to 500 by 1812. Father Cuesta would later brick up the archways connecting the side naves to the main nave of the church.

In 1833, the Mexican government passed the Secularization Act, which would result in the dissolution of the mission system by compelling them to sell off all their landholdings. Though the act would not be ratified

and implemented until 1834, initial changes began at Mission San Juan Bautista in 1833. In that year, the Mexican governor José Figueroa moved to replace the Spanish-born Franciscans at the missions in the northern part of Alta California with Zacatecan Franciscans who were part of a new generation born in the Western Hemisphere. Their tenure would be short-lived. Mission San Juan Bautista would be secularized in 1835 and placed under the control of a civilian administrator, a local landowner named José Tiburcio Castro. Father Cuesta left the mission in 1833 and passed away in 1840. He is buried at Mission Santa Inés, where he probably lived out his final years.

Meanwhile, the Spanish settlement that had grown up outside the mission walls had grown into a substantial community that had come to be known as San Juan de Castro after José Tiburcio Castro. It would later be renamed as San Juan Bautista after the mission. For most of the nineteenth century, this town would be an important stage stop on the highway between Los Angeles and San Francisco that had evolved from El Camino Reál. The center of the town was a plaza that was faced on one side by the Mission San Juan Bautista monastery, opposite the adobe Castro House, which was constructed by Castro's son, José María, in 1841, when he became the Mexican prefect of this district of Alta California. A building on another side of the plaza would be owned by the famous restaurateur,

Above: This bronze bell at Mission San Juan Bautista celebrates El Camino Reál.
Opposite: The arcade that fronts the convento provides a cool respite on a warm summer day. The rich Salinas Valley farmland seen in the distance was once mission property.

Angelo Zanetta. Next door to the Castro House was the Plaza Hotel, which Zanetta would remodel in 1858 from the old Spanish barracks building that dated back to 1814. The entrance to the mission church was located at the north corner of this plaza.

In July 1846, during the Mexican War, the area was touched

by the conflict when a U.S. Navy force under Commodore John Drake Sloat landed at nearby Monterey—claiming Alta California for the United States—and in November, U.S. Army Colonel John C. Frémont briefly used San Juan Bautista as his headquarters. Frémont had been to the area on a scouting mission in

Above: This conference room in the convento captures some of the mood of life during Mission San Juan Bautista's golden age.
Opposite: In this view looking toward the main altar in the primary nave, we can see the archways that lead to the two parallel side naves.

March of that year, and had been involved in a brief standoff with José María Castro at nearby Gavilan Peak.

In 1847, Patrick and Margaret Breen and their family arrived in San Juan Bautista after having spent more than three months of the previous winter starving in the snowdrifts of the Sierra Nevada with the Donner Party. At first, the destitute Breens took refuge at the mission, but later prospered and bought the Castro House, as well as extensive farmland in the San Juan Valley.

Though the title to the mission church would not be officially restored to the Catholic Church until 1859, it would continue to serve as a parish church for the town of San Juan Bautista through the years. By the 1860s, as the cities and towns in the new state of California flourished, so too did the Catholic parishes. As this happened, there was a tendency to modernize the churches. As would be the case at Mission San Luis Obispo de Tolosa and elsewhere, a wood-frame campanario with a pointed steeple was constructed at Mission San Juan Bautista.

In 1876, the fortunes of the thriving community suddenly reversed. When the Southern Pacific Railroad bypassed the town, the importance of San Juan Bautista as a stage stop suddenly faded. For the next half-century, it practically became a ghost town. During that time, a devastating earthquake occurred on the San Andreas Fault. The Great Earthquake of April 18, 1906, was centered north of San Francisco, but the proximity of Mission San Juan Bautista to the fault line meant that there was considerable harm done to the old mission church. Only the center nave would be used for the next four decades.

In 1933, the town of San Juan Bautista enjoyed a bit of a renaissance when the State of California formally designated the old plaza area as the San Juan Bautista State Historic Park. The Castro House, as well as the various Zanetta properties and other buildings, were dusted off and eventually restored to their mid-nineteenth-century splendor. In 1949, it was the turn of Mission San Juan Bautista. William Randolph Hearst had taken an interest in the old missions, especially Mission San Antonio de Padua, but the Hearst Foundation would also make a generous grant to Mission San Juan Bautista. Over the coming years, the mission church, including the side naves, would be restored and a new adobe campanario built. Steel girders were hidden in the walls for earthquake protection. Today, the restored mission church at Mission San Juan Bautista continues to serve as an active parish church within the Diocese of Monterey.

CHAPTER SIXTEEN

MISSION SAN MIGUEL ARCÁNGEL

THE SIXTEENTH MISSION IN THE Alta California mission chain, Mission San Miguel Arcángel was the third of the four missions founded by Father Fermín Lasuén during his busy summer of 1797. It was located on El Camino Reál at a place previously selected in 1795, near a village of the Salinan people known as Cholame, or Chulam, and near where the Nacimiento River flows into the Salinas River. The present California town of Cholame is located about twenty-five miles east of San Miguel Arcángel.

In keeping with Father Lasuén's plan to fill in the spaces along El Camino Reál to make it so that the missions would be about a day's ride apart, Mission San Miguel Arcángel was situated about halfway between Mission San Luis Obispo de Tolosa and Mission San Antonio de Padua. Its formal dedication took place on July 25, 1797, just a month after that of Mission San Juan Bautista. According to various reports, between fifteen and twenty-five

Salinan neophytes were baptized on the first day.

Father Lasuén named the new mission for St. Michael the Archangel, who is, along with St. Gabriel and St. Raphael, one of three archangels venerated by the Catholic Church. Mission San Miguel Arcángel would be the second of the three Alta California missions dedicated to the archangels. The defender of both Christians and Jews, St. Michael is mentioned in both the Old and New Testaments of the Bible, specifically in the books of Daniel, Jude, and Revelation. He is usually depicted in art clad in armor and holding a sword, ready to do battle with the devil and enemies of the faith.

The first Franciscan administrator assigned to Mission San Miguel Arcángel was Father Buenaventura Sitjar, who had spent the previous quarter-century working with the Salinan people as senior missionary at Mission San Antonio de Padua. He spoke the various dialects of their language, and had a good rapport with them. He soon returned to San

Above: This oxcart that delights fourth-grade visitors to Mission San Miguel is representative of the types of vehicles that once passed by the missions on El Camino Reál. Opposite: The convento arcade and fountain, with the church beyond.

Antonio de Padua and was succeeded by Father Juan Martín, who would serve until his death in 1824.

The missionaries and the neophytes moved quickly. Construction work on the structures for Mission

San Miguel Arcángel was underway immediately, and the first mud-roofed adobe church was finished in 1798. The mission quadrangle was complete two years later, and the fields, pastures, orchards, and vineyard were

planted and irrigated. Things had gone so well that the Franciscans began thinking about an asistencia, or satellite mission, to the east in the Tulare Valley. In November 1804, contact was made with people living in this area at a village called Bubal. They seemed receptive to the missionaries and plans were put in motion for building an asistencia here. However, the people at Bubal were involved in a quarrel with another group of people and this disagreement turned violent. Spanish soldiers became involved in the fight, angering both sides, and the Franciscans were unable to mediate the disagreement. Against this backdrop, the asistencia plan was shelved and never revived.

After 1806, the mission would have higher priorities closer to home. In that year, a major fire gutted the mission complex, destroying the church and goods that had been in the storerooms, such as tools and food supplies, as well as leather, cloth, and stocks of wool. As would occur nearly two centuries later, in the wake of the 2003 earthquake, the neighboring missions came to the immediate aid of Mission San Miguel.

Father Martín would wait ten years before beginning construction of a new, permanent tile-roofed church, but workshops, storerooms, living spaces, and the granary would be rebuilt within two years. Also during the intervening decade, a large stockpile of adobe bricks and clay roof tiles would be manufactured in preparation for the church construction.

Above: Mission San Miguel as it appeared in about 1899. The mission church and convento were still intact, but the building at the right, which was located in front of the cemetery, had collapsed. This building was removed and never replaced.
Opposite: The facade of the mission church as it appeared in December 2001, two years before the devastating earthquake.

Contact Information:
MISSION SAN MIGUEL ARCÁNGEL
775 Mission Street, P.O. Box 69
San Miguel, CA 93451
Phone: (805) 467-2131
Museum/Gift shop:
(805) 467-3256

Web site:
www.missionsanmiguel.org
E-mail:
friars@missionsanmiguel.org

In October 1807, Father Martín was joined at Mission San Miguel Arcángel by Father Juan Cabot, who would remain at the mission until 1819, and return as senior missionary after Father Martín's death in 1824. Father Cabot's brother, Pedro Cabot, was a Franciscan stationed at Mission San Antonio de Padua at about the same time.

Despite the fire and its aftermath, Mission San Miguel Arcángel was flourishing. By the time that Father Cabot arrived, there were a thousand neophytes living at the mission. Through the end of 1832, a total of 2,471 baptisms and 764 weddings had been performed at the mission. This was roughly the same as would be performed at nearby Mission San Luis Obispo de Tolosa, which predated San Miguel Arcángel by a quarter-century.

Though there would never be an asistencia, records show that Mission San Miguel Arcángel constructed a number of houses at satellite locations, probably in connection with agricultural operations such as grazing. Technically, the mission lands encompassed more than 3,600 square miles, extending from the Pacific Ocean, thirty-five miles west of the mission, to a line more than a hundred miles inland. One structure was built overlooking the Pacific Ocean near present-day San Simeon, and two years later, another was built on El Camino Reál near what is now Atascadero.

In about 1813, Father Cabot is credited with having developed a small settlement near a sulfur hot springs about eight miles south of Mission San Miguel Arcángel. He noticed that the native people were bathing in the naturally steamy waters to relieve the arthritis that they suffered during cold, damp weather. He called it Rancho El Paso de Robles, built a shelter and a wood lining for the pool, and promoted its use. Later in the nineteenth century, these hot mineral baths attracted visitors from throughout California and a town grew up around the springs. Initially called Hot Springs, the town was renamed Paso Robles in 1870. Interest in the springs waned in the early twentieth century, and the hot springs were plugged. During the 2003 earthquake, one of the hot springs burst open again in the parking lot of the Paso Robles City Hall.

At the mission, construction of the new permanent church began in 1816, working from the stone foundation that had been laid two years before. Because many of the building materials had been prepared ahead of

Above: The nave at the Mission San Miguel church. The all-seeing eye of God designed by Estévan Munras can be seen above the altar.
Opposite: The rustic old gate to the cemetery at Mission San Miguel.

time, work proceeded relatively quickly, and the church was finished by 1818. About two years later, a man named Estévan Carlos Munras came to Mission San Miguel Arcángel. He was a merchant who had arrived in Monterey in about 1812, and would go on to become an important landowner in the region. Munras was also the artist who would supervise the interior decoration of the church at Mission San Miguel Arcángel. Included in this work was the all-seeing eye of God that is on the reredos above the old high altar.

There are a number of versions of the story of how Estévan Munras came to Mission San Miguel Arcángel, and when he painted the church. Some stories say that he had known Father Martín in Barcelona, and others have him as a friend of Father Cabot. The latter would appear unlikely, because Father Cabot was not at Mission San Miguel Arcángel between 1819 and 1824, when the interior was probably being painted. Munras may have started the work as early as 1820, but he was probably finished by 1824. In the meantime, he

married Catalina Manzanelli, who some sources identify as the daughter of a silk merchant from Genoa in Italy. The wedding occurred, however, at Mission Nuestra Señora de la Soledad, not at Mission San Miguel Arcángel. Munras would later serve as alcalde of Monterey, where, today, one of the major thoroughfares in the center of the city is named for him.

In 1824, Father Martín passed away, and in November, Father Cabot returned as senior missionary at Mission San Miguel Arcángel. He would remain for exactly ten years,

until November 1834. It was on Father Cabot's watch that secularization would come to Mission San Miguel Arcángel. As a prelude, Mexican Governor José María de Echeandía had decreed that the neophytes could leave the missions, but it is reported that none left Mission San Miguel Arcángel. The mission was finally secularized in July 1836, with Ignacio Coronel named as civilian administrator of the property. Father Ramón Abella, who arrived at the mission after Father Cabot departed, would remain until his death in 1841. A small number of neophytes would also stay on at the mission quadrangle, but gradually the infrastructure fell into disrepair. There would not be a priest in residence at Mission San Miguel Arcángel again for nearly three decades. On an 1842 inspection trip to Mission San Miguel Arcángel, Father-President Narciso Durán noted that the mission was a virtual ghost town, with the neophytes having been "demoralized and dispersed."

In 1846, shortly before the United States took possession of Alta California, Governor Pío Pico began selling off the last of the mission properties. At Mission San Miguel Arcángel, he sold most of the quadrangle to Petronillo Rios and William Reed for $600, or about $12,000 in today's dollars. Reed moved into a wing of the quadrangle with his family and their servants. Within a week of Reed's purchase, Alta California became part of the United States, and three years later the gold rush brought swarms of immigrants, many of them unsavory characters bent on getting rich the easy way—by stealing gold from those who had acquired it the hard way.

Meanwhile, El Camino Reál had become a busy highway between Los Angeles and San Francisco. The former Mission San Miguel Arcángel had been designed as a natural stopping place on that route and it remained so. In 1849, five nefarious individuals stopping at the mission overheard the people living there talking about gold. That night, Reed and his entire family were murdered, but the would-be thieves found no gold. A posse caught up with the killers near the Pacific Ocean. One was shot in a gun battle and another fell to his death trying to escape. The other three were captured, tried, and executed at Santa Barbara. Tales are still told of the mission being haunted by the spirits of the Reed family.

During the decade after the Reed murders, the property was used for a time as a hotel and saloon. Through it all, the interior of the church, including Estévan Munras's artwork, remained relatively intact. In 1859, the mission was finally restored to the Catholic Church by order of President James Buchanan, but it was not until 1878 that Father Philip Farrelly became the first resident priest at Mission San Miguel Arcángel since Father Abella passed away thirty-seven years earlier.

A half-century later, in 1928, the Franciscan Order returned to stay. The church would continue to function as a parish church under the Franciscans, who would also operate a novitiate and retreat residence at the site. Unlike most of the other missions along this section of El Camino Reál, the town of San Miguel that grew up around Mission San Miguel Arcángel would remain small.

Because it suffered less from the ordeal of faulty restoration projects, the mission itself would continue through the end of the twentieth century to pride itself on being one of California's best-preserved and most authentic missions, and an important reminder of California's past.

Throughout the annals of the California missions, earthquakes have played a role in abruptly altering the course of the history of individual missions. On December 22, 2003, it was the turn of Mission San Miguel Arcángel. An earthquake measuring 6.5 on the Richter scale rumbled through several Central Coast communities, collapsing buildings in Paso Robles and doing severe damage to the structures at Mission San Miguel Arcángel, especially to the venerable mission church.

Two days later, after a lengthy inspection by engineers, the pastor, Father Raymond Tintle, made the decision to close the church, front courtyard, and cemetery in the interest of public safety. Casa San Miguel, also located in the town of San Miguel, granted the mission parish the use of their facilities for the mission Mass services. On December 31, Kevin Drabinski, the director of communications for the Diocese of Monterey, announced that San Luis Obispo County had "red-tagged" the church property, meaning that it could not be occupied.

A team of professional engineers and architects evaluated the earthquake damage, and on January 15, 2004, Mission San Miguel Arcángel reopened its parish office, gift shop, and museum to the public. While the old mission church remained closed, Father Tintle observed that "We're open for business and on the mend . . . There's so much history, pathos and spirituality encompassed in these old walls, that they're as much part of the structure as the adobe brick! It would be a sin to let this all crumble away."

On February 13, the New World Baroque Orchestra, under the direction of John Warren, performed a benefit concert for San Miguel Arcángel at Mission San Luis Obispo de Tolosa as part of the annual conference of the California Mission Studies Association. On May 30, 2004, St. Rose of Lima Church in Paso Robles hosted another such musical event that brought together ten area churches.

In April, TWG Construction of Torrance, California, had completed a critical stage of the stabilization and restoration of the historic church of Mission San Miguel with the installation of emergency shoring at critical

Above: The colorful arcade at the convento. The museum is located inside.
Opposite: The garden within the quadrangle at Mission San Miguel on a brisk winter day.

points in the earthquake-damaged structure. Shoring was added to the window above the front door and inside the front door itself. Other reinforcement included buttressing the north sacristy wall to keep it from falling down and potentially affecting the stability of the entire north side of the church itself. TWG also shored the windows on the south wall and buttressed the arcade on each end and two of the arches within the arcade. This was merely a stabilization effort designed to prevent further damage. The full restoration would take several years to complete.

CHAPTER SEVENTEEN

MISSION SAN FERNANDO REY DE ESPAÑA

K NOWN AS PASHECGNA TO the native peoples of the region, the location that was chosen for the seventeenth mission was well known to the Franciscans. When Father Juan Crespí had passed this way with the expedition of Gaspar de Portolá in 1769, he had named the area La Valle de Santa Catalina de Bolonia de los Encinos, or St. Catherine of Bologna's Valley of the Live Oaks. St. Catherine's Valley was on El Camino Reál, roughly halfway between Mission San Gabriel Arcángel and Mission San Buenaventura, and it had been passed many times by missionaries and traders using this increasingly busy thoroughfare. It was an ideal site both in terms of its location on the Royal Road and in terms of the availability of land and water. Unfortunately, it was also claimed by Don Francisco Reyes, the alcalde of the pueblo of Los Angeles, as his Rancho Encino. The claim might have been challenged legally, but before it became an issue, Reyes graciously offered to donate the

property to the church. He was listed as a patron at the dedication ceremony and he offered himself as the godfather of the first child to be baptized at the mission.

Father Fermín Lasuén presided over the formal dedication of Mission San Fernando Rey de España on September 8, 1797, just six weeks after he had dedicated Mission San Miguel Arcángel. It was his fourth mission in less that three months. It was named not for St. Catherine, but for St. Ferdinand, who had ruled the Spanish kingdoms of Leon and Castile in the thirteenth century as King Ferdinand III. Born near Salamanca in 1198, Ferdinand was the son of King Alfonso IX of Leon and of Berengeria, the daughter of King Alfonso III of Castile. Berengeria's sister was Blanche, the mother of France's King Louis IX, who became St. Louis, the namesake of the next Alta California mission to be founded by Father Lasuén.

Ferdinand became king of Castile in 1217, and in 1230 he took

Above: The old mission church as photographed by Henry Withey in April 1934. Opposite: One of two once located in the quadrangle at Mission San Fernando, this fountain is based on the design of a fountain located in Cordova, a Spanish city once ruled by King Ferdinand III, the mission's namesake. The mission church is in the background.

the crown of Leon, uniting the two kingdoms. In 1219, he married Beatrice, the daughter of Philip of Swabia, the king of Germany, and they had seven children. During his reign, Ferdinand was responsible for

evicting the Moorish invaders from much of what is now Spain, including Cordova and Seville. In these areas, he built churches, founded monasteries, endowed hospitals, and established the University of Salamanca. When he

died in Seville in May 1252, Ferdinand was buried in the great cathedral in that city. Many miracles are said to have taken place at his tomb, and Pope Clement X canonized him in 1671.

The missionaries, Spanish soldiers, and neophytes went to work on the construction of the first church at Mission San Fernando Rey de España, living in the relative comfort of Don Francisco Reyes' nearby ranch house. The church was completed in 1799, but was replaced by a much larger building one year later, and by a third church in 1806. Finished at about the turn of the century, the quadrangle measured 295 feet by 315 feet. In addition, a convento was constructed outside the quadrangle in later years to enclose guest rooms and other facilities. It was 243 feet in length. Guest rooms were important as Mission San Fernando Rey de España gradually became an important way station on El Camino Reál.

The progressively larger churches constructed at Mission San Fernando Rey de España itself were necessitated by the rapidly growing neophyte population, which had reached an estimated one thousand by 1804. Through the end of 1832, a total of 2,784 baptisms and 827 weddings had been performed at Mission San Fernando Rey de España. This data compares to 7,825 baptisms and 1,916 weddings that were performed though 1832 at the neighboring Mission San Gabriel Arcángel, which had already been active for twenty-six years before San Fernando Rey de España was established.

Above: A weathered marble cherub in the garden at Mission San Fernando.
Right: An old gnarled fruit tree in the mission quadrangle. Many of the fruits and vegetables that are now an important part of California's agriculture were originally introduced here in the eighteenth century by the Franciscan missionaries.
Opposite: The mission church today.

Contact Information:
MISSION SAN FERNANDO REY DE ESPAÑA

15151 San Fernando Mission Blvd.
Mission Hills, CA 93145
Mission: (818) 361-0186
Archdiocese Archival Center:
Phone: (818) 365-1501
Fax: (818) 361-3276

The neophytes were drawn from the native Tongva people who lived throughout what is now the San Fernando Valley. Though the Tongva living near Mission San Fernando Rey de España would be called Fernandeño by the Spanish, they were closely related to the Tongva people known as Gabrieleño at Mission San Gabriel Arcángel. The language spoken by the Tongva is classed by linguists as Shoshonean, making the Tongva linguistic relatives of the Shoshone people who lived through-out the Great Basin country of what is now Nevada, Utah, and Idaho. There may also have been some Chumash people from the coastal areas near Mission San Buenaventura living at Mission San Fernando Rey de España.

Like Mission San Gabriel Arcángel, Mission San Fernando Rey de España is remembered for the substantial trade that it conducted with the growing pueblo of Los Angeles during the early years of the nineteenth century. At its peak in 1819, the mission grazed nearly 22,000 head of cattle on its 190 square miles of land. From this, large quantities of soap, hides, and finished leather goods were produced, and these found a ready market in Los Angeles and elsewhere. In addition, those 190 square miles are recorded to have contained 30,000 grape vines, the wine from which would also have been popular in Los Angeles. Olive oil was another important cash crop, and specialized crafts such as wood and ironwork were also trademarks of Mission San Fernando Rey de España.

Above: The immaculately manicured mission grounds. One of the mission bells can be seen in the church's campanario in the center.
Opposite: This arcade fronts the section of the quadrangle that once housed the saddlery. The church is in the background.

In terms of production of wheat, corn, and other field crops, Mission San Fernando Rey de España was about average for the missions of its region. Its annual average of 136 tons was equal to that of Mission San Luis Rey and Mission San Buenaventura, while being ahead of the Mission San Juan Capistrano average of eighty-four tons and substantially behind the 234 tons averaged at Mission San Gabriel Arcángel. Because the warmer and drier environment was better for

wheat, Mission San Fernando Rey de España ranked second among the southern missions with an average of 113 tons, compared to 128 tons for Mission San Gabriel Arcángel.

Among the important outposts that were constructed on the Mission San Fernando Rey de España lands was the satellite mission known as Asistencia San Francisco Javier. It was constructed in 1804 near the Santa Clara River and Castaic Creek in the mountains north of the mission. Originally, the building was used to

house ranch hands, but later it served as a small chapel.

A major setback to the evolution of Mission San Fernando Rey de España would come in the form of the two earthquakes that occurred in December 1812, both of which measured with an estimated magnitude of 7.0 on the Richter scale. The Wrightwood Earthquake on December 8 destroyed the Great Stone Church at Mission San Juan Capistrano and did severe damage to buildings at Mission San Fernando Rey de España. Two

weeks later, the December 21 earthquake ruined the churches at both Mission San Buenaventura and Mission San Fernando Rey de España, which were just three and six years old at the time of the earthquake.

Though the infrastructure at Mission San Fernando Rey de España would be rebuilt, the earthquakes essentially marked an early end to the mission's golden age. The neophyte population had already begun to dwindle, and the physical collapse of the mission did little to curtail the overall decline. Meanwhile, neighboring settlements were growing and gradually encroaching on mission lands. A decade after the earthquakes, Mexico's independence from Spain brought an end to official government support for the missions, and a decade after that, secularization brought an end to the mission system as it had been known. Father Ibarra, the mission's senior missionary, stayed on for about a year after San Fernando Rey de España was secularized in 1834, but finally threw up his hands in disgust at the meddling of the local government, and the mission was abandoned. Both the mission and its little San Francisco Javier asistencia would go through the hands of a series of private owners and squatters.

Discoveries of deposits of naturally occurring gold would define the nineteenth-century history of California after 1848, but the first California gold rush is scarcely remembered. Occurring in 1842,

Above: A porcelain plaque depicting Nuestra Señora de Montserrat, Our Lady of Montserrat. The Spanish city of Montserrat had been a center of pilgrimage to the Blessed Virgin since the tenth century. Opposite: The main altar and the great golden reredos of Mission San Fernando.

the first gold rush in the Golden State would directly impact Mission San Fernando Rey de España. A cattle rancher named Don Francisco Lopéz discovered a placer, or streambed gold deposit, while he was digging wild onions in a place called San Feliciano Canyon, north of the mission near present-day Newhall. This area, which became known as Placeritas Canyon, was soon swarming with gold seekers. The gold rush

would continue for a couple of years, and many individuals, notably a Los Angeles businessman named Antonio Coronel, invested a great deal in mining operations. In one of the darker moments of the gold rush, a rumor spread that the missionaries had known about the gold and that they had buried some at the mission. This led to an unauthorized and disorganized search of the mission that left many of the surviving buildings in almost as bad a shape as they had been after the earthquakes three decades earlier.

In 1845, when Governor Pío Pico began selling off mission churches, the complex at Mission San Fernando Rey de España came into the hands of his brother Andres Pico. The latter hastened to leave the mission a year later when the U.S. Army arrived in the San Fernando Valley. As he had at other missions in the north, Colonel John Frémont used the facilities at Mission San Fernando Rey de España as his headquarters for a while.

In 1861, the title to Mission San Fernando Rey de España was returned to the Catholic Church, but the property was in such poor shape that it was not reoccupied for use as a church. The large convento, by then the only useful building left standing, was used for a variety of purposes. Records indicate that it was being used as a hog barn in 1896.

It was about this time that the old mission came to the attention of

Charles Fletcher Lummis. A colorful individual who became a well-known Los Angeles character at the turn of the century, Lummis had been the first city editor of the *Los Angeles Times*, and had become a crusader for American Indian rights while living in New Mexico. In 1897, he founded the Landmarks Club of Southern California, one of the first organizations in the United States dedicated to historic preservation.

Lummis was a man on a mission, and his mission was, simply put, to save the missions of Southern California. He raised the money necessary to stabilize and restore such deteriorating institutions as Mission San Juan Capistrano and Mission San Fernando Rey de España.

He used the 1897 centennial of Mission San Fernando Rey de España to raise money for a new roof. In 1916, Lummis and the Landmarks Club organized the San Fernando Candle Day, a visually spectacular publicity event. An estimated 6,000 people paid a dollar each to carry candles through the venerable arcades of Mission San Fernando Rey de España.

By 1923, the mission church at San Fernando Rey de España was completely rebuilt and functioning once again, this time under the pastorship of the Oblate Fathers.

Unfortunately, the nearly forgotten San Francisco Javier asistencia was completely torn apart during the early twentieth century by treasure hunters still following the tales of

gold that had been buried by the missionaries.

On February 9, 1971, 159 years after it had been devastated by a pair of earthquakes, Mission San Fernando Rey de España was struck again. Measuring 6.7 on the Richter scale, the Sylmar Earthquake hit the San Fernando Valley at 6:01 in the morning, killing sixty-five people and collapsing buildings and freeways. At San Fernando Rey de España, the mission church was so badly harmed that it would not be fully restored until 1974. Fortunately, the church would survive a series of temblors that rumbled through the San Fernando Valley later in the twentieth century, including the Northridge Earthquake on January 17, 1994, which also measured 6.7 on the Richter scale.

With a large sixteenth-century reredos having been installed in the church in 1991, Mission San Fernando Rey de España is one of the important historical sites in Southern California. Because of its proximity to Hollywood, it has also starred in numerous films through the years. Once a major crossroads along El Camino Reál, the mission is now located within a mile or so of three of Southern California's busiest thoroughfares, the Golden State Freeway (Interstate 5), the San Diego Freeway (Interstate 405), and the Simi Valley Freeway (California Route 118). The mission is now also home to the Archival Center for the Archdiocese of Los Angeles.

CHAPTER EIGHTEEN

MISSION SAN LUIS REY DE FRANCIA

During 1797, Father Fermín Lasuén had established four new missions in rapid succession in his effort to fill in the gaps along the central part of El Camino Reál so that the missions in the Alta California system were conveniently located a day's ride apart. In the summer of 1798, he returned to this project, locating a mission midway between what were then the two southernmost of the chain. This new mission, the eighteenth in the mission system, would be roughly centered between Mission San Diego de Alcalá and Mission San Juan Capistrano. The proximity to San Diego was important to the new mission because the missionaries could utilize the port facilities there to import supplies from New Spain.

The site chosen for the mission was known in the Takic dialect of the native people of the region as Tacayme, while the broad east-to-west valley in which it lay was known as Quechinga. As was the case with most of the 1797 missions, the site had been well known

since Gaspar de Portolá had made his 1769 expedition to the north from Mission San Diego. Since it was just a day's ride north of San Diego, missionaries had passed it many times over the three decades before a mission finally graced this hill.

Father Lasuén formally dedicated the mission on June 13, 1798, almost exactly one year after Mission San José, the first of the four 1797 missions. It would, however, be the only mission added to the system in 1798 and the last mission to be added for six years. He named it Mission San Luis Rey de Francia after St. Louis, who had reigned as King Louis IX of France in the thirteenth century. He was a contemporary of St. Ferdinand, who had reigned as King Ferdinand III of Spain. Indeed, the only two monarchs to become namesakes of Alta California missions were also cousins—their mothers were sisters.

St. Louis was born at Poissy in France on April 25, 1215, the son of Louis VIII of France and Blanche of

Above: Candles blaze inside the mission's Madonna Chapel, dedicated to the Virgin Mary.
Opposite: The arcade leads into the mission church, the largest in the mission chain.

Castile. He became king at the age of eleven upon the death of his father, although Blanche would rule France as regent for many years. In 1234, Louis IX married Marguerite of Provence, with whom he would have eleven children. As king, Louis IX would lead

two crusades, those of 1248–1249 and 1270. In the meantime, he entered negotiations with Henry III to secure a treaty to preclude further warfare between France and England. In the Treaty of Paris, signed in May 1258, the two sides agreed to trade land that

they occupied and to stop fighting. England received areas including Limoges, while France gained sovereignty over lands such as Normandy and Anjou.

Louis IX is said to have been both a pious man and just with his subjects, and he earned a reputation as an equitable international mediator. He is also recalled for having built one of the supreme masterpieces of Gothic architecture, Sainte Chapelle in Paris, as a reliquary for a relic that was reputed to be the Crown of Thorns worn by Jesus Christ at the Crucifixion. He was also a patron of the Sorbonne University. He died near Tunis on August 25, 1270, and was canonized for leading the Crusades by Pope Boniface VIII in 1297, 501 years prior to the founding of the Alta California mission that would be named for him.

More than simply having been named for a king, Mission San Luis Rey de Francia was itself known as the "King of Missions," in part because it would soon evolve as both the largest and most prosperous of all the missions. Under the direction of Father Antonio Peyri, who would serve as senior missionary at the mission for thirty-four years, the mission infrastructure expanded rapidly. Several buildings were built within the first year, and the original adobe mission was completed in 1802.

In 1811, work began on the permanent mission church of Mission San Luis Rey de Francia. It would be 138 feet long, making it larger than any other mission church in the southern part of Alta California except the Great Stone Church at Mission San Juan Capistrano. Ironically, this church would be destroyed just a year later in the December 8, 1812, earthquake. When it was dedicated in 1815, the church at Mission San Luis Rey de Francia would be the largest in the region.

According to the National Park Service historical survey work done at the mission in 1937, the church was constructed of adobe on a foundation of fieldstone probably laid in lime mortar. The altars and arches, pilasters, moldings, and the campanario were made of brick and plastered over. So too was the dome that was added in 1829. The roof was framed with timbers and covered with clay tiles. Also completed between 1811 and 1815, the quadrangle would measure roughly 500 feet on a side and contain quarters for the missionaries, as well as a granary, shops, storerooms, and other living areas.

As it was at all the missions, agriculture was essential to survival, and water management was essential to agriculture. The mission was established near a marsh, and two dams were constructed. The reservoirs were used to collect sufficient water for irrigating a garden near the quadrangle. Father Peyri best summarized this situation when he later wrote that "although there is an arroyo which runs down from the

Sierra Madre [San Luis Rey River], it has abundant water only in the rainy season, from the month of October or November to May or June of the next year, when it is again lost in the sand, so that, the arroyo being then dry, we can not count on it for any seed time."

In terms of a comparison with other missions, the King of Missions is remembered for the immense herds of livestock that it ran on ranchos throughout the vast mission lands east of the mission complex. At the end of 1832, the mission had a total of 57,330 head of livestock, more than twice the 26,342 head at second-place Mission San Fernando Rey de España. This included 27,500 head of cattle, a 22 percent increase over 1827. The inventory of 26,100 head of sheep in 1832

represented a 2 percent increase over 1831, although it was down slightly from the 27,412 head of sheep that were in the mission's herd in 1827. The number of goats increased from 1,120 to 1,300 between 1827 and 1832, and the number of horses climbed from 1,501 to 1,950. The fact that the numbers were increasing at this time, which was toward the end of the mission era and well past the golden age of Mission San Luis Rey de Francia, makes the figures especially impressive. The huge livestock herds would have also made Mission San Luis Rey de Francia a force to be reckoned with in the leather trade. San Luis Rey de Francia is also known to have been an important source of soap, blankets, and shoes for the settlements in and around San Diego as well as in its own area.

As for field crop production, Mission San Luis Rey de Francia was about average for the region. The annual production of wheat, barley, corn, and other crops stood at 136 tons, equal to Mission San Fernando Rey de España and Mission San Buenaventura, but between the 158 tons at Mission San Diego and the eighty-four tons at Mission San Juan Capistrano. In terms of wheat, the

primary field crop at all of the missions, Mission San Luis Rey de Francia averaged just thirty-nine tons, less than any of the southern missions. Through 1832, the mission produced 26,452 tons of wheat and 66,204 tons of other crops. It its final years, however, San Luis Rey de Francia is said to have had an annual output of 2,500 barrels of wine. Although Mission San Diego de Alcalá may have outproduced Mission San Luis Rey de Francia on average through the years, Father Peyri noted in 1827 that his mission was supplying corn, beans, and wheat to the Presidio of San Diego.

Most of the missions with agricultural operations on widely separated plots of land constructed outposts and ranch houses on them. According to a report penned by Father Peyri, cattle were run on land about eight miles east of the mission, and a sheep ranch was located further out in the same direction. About thirty miles to the northeast was another mission cattle ranch called Rancho de San Jacinto. As Father Peyri described it, the reason for their being so scattered was the need for water for both fields and pastures. He added that such was the case for other missions and settlements all along the coast region. "Necessity compels searching for both in the [canyons] which the Sierra Madre offers for the planting of grain as well as for pastures for the livestock," he wrote in 1827, "so that we may be able to maintain in community the native converts."

In some cases, the missions specifically established satellite missions, or asistencias, at these distant locations. In the case of Mission San Luis Rey de Francia, there would be two sites that are identified as having been asistencias. The first was Asistencia San Antonio de Pala, which was located in a wooded, mountainous area east of San Luis Rey de Francia, about twenty-five miles inland from the Pacific Ocean. Father Peyri formally dedicated this asistencia in June 1816, although the mission had an outpost here as early as 1810 that served as a headquarters for a farm where grain and beans were being grown. As he described this site, it had "a church, dwellings, and granaries and with a few fields where wheat, corn, beans, garbanzos, and other leguminous plants are grown. There are also a vineyard and an orchard of various fruits and of olives, for which there is sufficient irrigation, the water being from the stream [the San Luis Rey River] which runs to the vicinity of this mission."

Another satellite operation of Mission San Luis Rey de Francia was located north of the mission and closer to El Camino Reál and was referred to by Father Peyri as "Rancho de San Pedro, known as Las Flores." He described Las Flores as having a house, granaries, and a chapel, which formed a square or large patio. He also noted that "In the patio, by means of water taken out of a pool near the sea, corn is raised. In the plain, wheat and barley are raised in season." About three miles from the rancho were cattle pastures at a place called Las Pulgas. There has been some question whether or not this location may have been formally dedicated as an asistencia, but the fact that Father Peyri confirmed that Mass was said at the chapel indicates that it probably was.

Statistically, Mission San Luis Rey de Francia was also about average in terms of the number of neophytes living at the mission. Beginning with fifty-four children baptized the first day, a total of 5,399 baptisms were performed at the mission through 1832, along with 1,335 weddings. Of all the Southern California missions, only San Diego, San Gabriel Arcángel, and Santa Bárbara had more. Mission San Diego had 6,522 baptisms and 1,794 weddings, although it was in service for nearly twice as many years.

The neophytes were drawn mainly from the local people whom the Spanish referred to as Luiseño, after the mission. Previously, these people had been called Payomkawichum, meaning "westerners," by the people living to the east, and their name for themselves was Ataaxum, which meant "people." The Luiseño shared the Takic dialect of the Uto-Aztecan language with their neighbors, the Acjachemen people, whom the Spanish would call Juaneño because they lived near Mission San Juan Capistrano.

Like the Juaneño, and like the Yuman-speaking Kumeyaay people to the south, the Luiseño were hunter-gatherers. They hunted wild game, such as quail, deer, and rabbits, and they gathered the acorns from the oak trees throughout Southern California's coastal mountain ranges.

When Mexico assumed control of Alta California from Spain in 1822, Father Peyri declared his allegiance to the new government, hoping for a seamless transition for Mission San Luis Rey de Francia as the political winds changed direction. However, as it became obvious that Mexico planned ultimately to secularize the missions, he tendered his resignation and left what had been his home for more than three decades. Father Peyri had become so well liked at the mission that when he departed, an estimated 500 neophytes waded into the surf at San Diego to bid farewell to his ship. Many had begged him to stay, and many would continue to pray for years that he would return to San Luis Rey de Francia someday.

One of the first missions to be secularized, Mission San Luis Rey de Francia continued to function as a

Above: The fountain is the centerpiece of the mission's inner gardens. Completed in 1903, the new quadrangle surrounding the garden is more compact than the original. Opposite: This arch is the last major remnant of the old quadrangle's arcade. These gardens contain the oldest pepper tree in California, brought from Peru in about 1830.

church until the buildings themselves were confiscated by Governor Pío Pico around the end of 1845 along with the asistencia at San Antonio de Pala. The other outpost at Las Flores was taken over by Pico and his brother in a separate land deal and incorporated into their Rancho Santa Margarita y Las Flores. In 1864, this property was

Above: The main entrance to the cemetery at Mission San Luis Rey de Francia. It contains a monument to the many neophytes buried here. Franciscan fathers are buried in a crypt beneath the campanario, which is entered by way of the cemetery. Opposite: In this view we see the main altar and a portion of the left side altar. Statues of St. Joseph and the Madonna are on either side of the old Mexican crucifix. The statue at the top of the center altar is of St. Louis (San Luis Rey). He is flanked by two archangels, St. Michael and St. Raphael.

sold to John Forster, the English-born brother-in-law of Pío Pico who had also bought Mission San Juan Capistrano.

In 1865, the Pico seizure of Mission San Luis Rey de Francia was finally reversed by the United States government and the mission was returned to the Catholic Church. However, it would remain in ruins for most of the balance of the nineteenth century. Finally, in 1892, a new pastor would arrive to revive the crumbling Mission San Luis Rey de Francia. Irish-born Father Joseph Jeremiah O'Keefe undertook the difficult task with an eye toward eventually turning the site into a seminary for Zacatecan Franciscans who were, by then, being forced to leave Mexico. The hardworking priest first prepared living quarters for the Zacatecan priests, of whom about two dozen would come to San Luis Rey de Francia. He began by rebuilding a wood-frame building for temporary housing at the front of the old mission church. He added a second two-story building that measured eighty-five feet by thirty-five feet.

Father O'Keefe decided to approach restoration of the mission church in stages because the roof and dome had collapsed, filling the interior with piles of debris. He would put off any work on the side chapel at the east side until 1913. He walled off the sanctuary on the north side and constructed his main altar here. He then put a heavily timbered drop ceiling in the nave so that the church could be used while restoration work was going on above and beyond the smaller space that he had blocked out. On May 13, 1893, Mission San Luis Rey de Francia was formally rededicated by Bishop Francis Mora. At the same time, the Apostolic College of Our Lady of Zacatecas opened on the mission grounds.

Over the next two decades, Father O'Keefe oversaw the systematic restoration of the mission church and the expansion of surrounding structures. With the church, his plan was in keeping with the mood of the early twentieth century in which the California missions were restored to their appearance during the mission era of a century before. New doors were added, holes were filled, new bells were hung in 1896 and 1901, and a new main altar installed in 1911. Old stairways from the church to the campanario and choir that had been filled in with adobe brick were discovered and repaired.

While the church was being restored, the quadrangle was rebuilt on a smaller scale than the original, with each side measuring 168 feet. The buildings on the quadrangle were occupied in 1903. The number of Zacatecans would decline gradually, and their place would be taken in 1912 by members of Father O'Keefe's own order, the Franciscan Province of the Sacred Heart, based in St. Louis, the Missouri city which shared the same patron saint as Mission San Luis Rey de Francia. Father O'Keefe himself retired from the mission in September 1912 and passed away at Mission Santa Bárbara on August 13, 1915.

Restoration work at Mission San Luis Rey de Francia did not stop with Father O'Keefe's departure. The dome of the church was rebuilt in 1930 under the direction of the Arizona-based architectural firm of Lescher and Mahony, and further work on the exterior was still ongoing a half-century later.

Meanwhile, the old Asistencia San Antonio de Pala was also undergoing its own restoration. It had gone through a series of private owners during the late nineteenth century, but in 1903 it was purchased by Charles Fletcher Lummis's Landmarks Club of Southern California and returned to the Catholic Church. Between 1954 and 1959, Father Januarius Carrillo supervised an extensive restoration project utilizing original materials. The other asistencia, at Las Flores, was on land taken by the U.S. Marine Corps during World War II, and is today on the grounds of Camp Pendleton. Las Flores has never been restored from the ruins into which it collapsed, but San Antonio de Pala has been a functioning church since 1959.

The grand church at Mission San Luis Rey de Francia, restored through the efforts of Father Joseph O'Keefe a century ago, now serves as a parish church and center for religious retreats and conferences.

Chapter Nineteen

Mission Santa Inés

BEFORE FATHER FERMÍN Lasuén passed away in 1803, he had essentially completed the task of establishing missions a day's ride apart along El Camino Reál, but there was still some interest in situating a nineteenth mission inland from Mission La Purísima Concepción between the homeland of the coastal Chumash people and their traditional rivals living in the inland valleys across the coastal mountain ranges that the Spanish referred to as Tulare. According to the records of the time, the Chumash had a favorable sentiment toward the missionaries, while the Tulare did not.

In 1798, the same year that Father Lasuén established Mission San Luis Rey de Francia, Captain Felipe de Goycoechea and Father Estévan Tápis surveyed sites for such a new mission in the Santa Ynez Valley east of La Purísima Concepción. Their survey essentially came down to two choices. These were a place known to the Chumash as Alajulapu, and another one called Calahuasa.

In 1803, Father Tápis assumed the office of father-president of the Alta California mission system upon the death of Father Fermín Lasuén that year. In 1804, he returned to the Santa Ynez Valley, specifically to Alajulapu. Reportedly, this location was picked at the urging of Governor José de Arrillaga because it was closer to El Camino Reál and thus more easily defended in times of emergency. It was also the more lightly populated of the two and thus offered more flexibility in setting up a new settlement. Though work on the buildings at the site began as early as March 1804, it was on September 17, 1804, that Father Tápis arrived to formally found his only mission. It would also be the only mission added to the Alta California mission system in the nearly two decades between 1798 and 1817. He named the first of the three nineteenth-century missions Mission Santa Inés.

The namesake of the new mission was St. Agnes of Assisi, the younger sister of St. Clare, and her

Above: An eighteenth-century statue of St. Agnes of Assisi (Santa Inés) stands atop the high altar of the mission for which she is the namesake.
Opposite: The cactus garden is situated before the arcade that leads to the mission church.

successor as abbess of the Poor Ladies. Born in Assisi in 1197 or 1198, Agnes was, like her sister, moved by the teachings and the example of St. Francis. Like Clare, Agnes left home to follow St. Francis, which angered her

father, Count Favorino. He sent his brother Monaldo and some soldiers to retrieve his younger daughter, but they found that they were unable to physically move her. They were, as it is described in Catholic legend, "over-

come by a spiritual power against which physical force availed not."

St. Francis was delighted by Agnes's heroic resistance to the threats and she became an important member of his inner circle. In 1219, he appointed her to head a new community of the Poor Ladies at Monticelli, near Florence. Agnes later established several such convents throughout northern Italy, including those at Mantua, Venice, and Padua. In 1253, Agnes was summoned to be at St. Clare's side as she neared death, and was present at her sister's funeral. Agnes herself would pass away on November 16 of the same year. Numerous miracles are said to have occurred at her tomb, and for this reason she was canonized by Pope Benedict XIV.

With the infrastructure having been under construction for half a year before Father Tápis formally dedicated Mission Santa Inés, things moved rather quickly. Much of the work was done by Chumash neophytes from neighboring missions. Supervising the work would be Father José Rumualdo Gutiérrez and Father José Antonio Calzada, who would be the first Franciscans stationed at Mission Santa Inés. Reportedly, a row of thick-walled adobe buildings 232 feet in length was mostly complete by the end of 1804. This included a temporary church that was roughly eighty-six feet long, a fourteen-foot sacristy, a granary that was 103 feet long, and quarters for the missionaries that measured twenty-

Above: The museum contains this bell, which was cast before the present church was dedicated in 1817.

Right: This painting from the mission's collection shows the campanario with three niches as it appeared in the nineteenth century and today. The campanario that existed between 1912 and 1948 had four.

Opposite: Inside the restored arcade.

Contact Information:
MISSION SANTA INÉS
1760 Mission Drive
P.O. Box 408
Solvang, CA 93464
Phone: (805) 688-4815
Fax: (805) 686-4468
Linea en español: (805) 688-6763

Web site:
www.missionsantaines.org
Online Gift Shop:
www.oldmissiongift.pointshop.com
Mission Office E-mail:
office@MissionSantaInes.org

nine feet. An additional 145-foot row would be in place by the end of 1805, and the Franciscans would report having completed 368 linear feet of new construction in 1806. When it was completed, each side of the mission quadrangle would measure 350 feet. A number of buildings outside the quadrangle were in place by 1810.

In December 1812, a pair of earthquakes measuring about 7.0 on the Richter scale slammed Southern California in the space of less than two weeks. The second one, centered near Santa Barbara, would cause considerable damage to Mission Santa Inés. In a contemporary report written by Father Francisco Javier de Uría and Father Olbes, two earthquakes occurred that morning within the space of fifteen minutes. "The first made a considerable aperture in one corner of the church; the second shock threw down the said corner, and a quarter of the new houses contiguous to the church collapsed to the foundation. All the thin walls of the upper houses fell down, demolished all the tiles, and opened a main wall. All remain serviceable, however, if no greater tremors occur."

Construction of a new and permanent church designed by Father Uría began the following year, and proceeded for four years. In the meanwhile, Father Uría designed an elaborate system of reservoirs and aqueducts to serve the needs of the mission. Also during this time, a second temporary church was constructed to the southeast of the quadrangle area, which was also undergoing reconstruction. Dedicated on July 4, 1817, the new church was twenty-five feet wide and measured 140 feet in length. Beginning a year after the church was completed, Father Uría directed an extensive mural painting project to enhance its interior. In 1824, a second such project gave us the adornment that is still visible within the Mission Santa Inés church at the beginning of the twenty-first century. This work included a statue of St. Agnes that is thought to have been created by a Chumash sculptor.

Father Uría not only built the church and rebuilt the quadrangle complex after the 1812 earthquake, he also can be credited with turning Mission Santa Inés into what may have been the most successful crop-producing mission in all of Alta California. The aqueduct system that he designed irrigated fields that produced a total of 8,986 tons of crops

Above and opposite: In 1926, the Capuchin Franciscans designed the hedge so that it formed a Celtic cross in the garden, with the fountain as the circular center element.

through 1832, more than any other mission except San Gabriel Arcángel, La Purísima Concepción, and Santa Clara de Asís—all of which were in operation much longer. In terms of annual average, Santa Inés was in the lead with 321 tons, compared to 318 tons at San José, 234 tons at San Gabriel Arcángel, and 212 tons at La Purísima Concepción. Santa Inés was second only to San Gabriel Arcángel in the production of wheat, the largest crop at any of the missions. San Gabriel Arcángel produced 6,386 tons between 1782 and 1832, while Santa Inés produced 6,304 tons between 1804 and 1832. The annual average was 128 tons for San Gabriel Arcángel and 225 tons at Santa Inés.

The livestock herds at Mission Santa Inés were also substantial, being second only to La Purísima Concepción among the missions of the central coast from Mission San Fernando Rey de España to Mission Santa Cruz. Between 1817, the year that the present church was dedicated, and 1832, on the eve of secularization, the number of cattle increased from 6,000 head to 7,200, although the number of sheep at the mission declined from about 5,000 to 2,100. The number of goats declined sharply from 120 to just twenty-eight, while the number of horses shrank by about half, from 770 to 390.

One of the most colorful characters from the folklore of Mission Santa Inés in the early nineteenth century was neither a missionary nor a neophyte, but rather a Yankee sailor who reached Alta California in the company of the notorious French buccaneer Hippolyte de Bouchard. As noted in the chapters on Mission San Buenaventura and Mission San Juan Capistrano, Bouchard created quite a bit of excitement along the California coast in the autumn of 1818. He came ashore to pillage Mission San Juan Capistrano, he attacked Monterey, and he threatened both Mission Santa Bárbara and Mission San Buenaventura.

At Santa Bárbara, he did not bother the mission, but he looted Rancho de Ortega in Refugio Canyon. Bouchard was surrounded here by Spanish soldiers, and in the ensuing firefight, several men from both sides were captured. Bouchard agreed to a prisoner exchange and was allowed to sail away. One man not exchanged was a seaman from Maine named Joseph Chapman, who had allegedly been shanghaied in Hawaii as a crewman aboard one of Bouchard's ships.

When he was released after imprisonment at the Presidio of Santa Bárbara, Chapman decided to remain in Alta California. He was baptized at Mission San Buenaventura, and went on to marry young Guadalupe Ortega—a daughter of the family who owned Rancho de Ortega— at Mission Santa Inés. Joseph and Guadalupe settled near Santa Inés, where, by 1821, he was employed by the missionaries to design various buildings, including a mill for process-

Above: The Mission Santa Inés campanario has been rebuilt several times, most recently in the late 1940s. The current configuration reflects the original 1817 appearance. Opposite: The mission church can be accessed from the garden through this side door.

ing the wool sheared from the mission's sheep.

In the early years, relations between the native Chumash and Mission Santa Inés had generally been good. The neophyte population is recorded to have stood at 920 in 1817, which was about average for the missions at that time. Most missions were recording around a thousand neophytes during the second decade of the nineteenth century, after which the number began to decline sharply.

Beginning with twenty-seven Chumash children baptized on the first day in 1804, a total of 1,030 baptisms would be performed at the mission through 1817, while only 318 would be recorded in the fifteen years following 1817. There would be 287 marriages between 1804 and 1817, and 113 between 1818 and 1832. Joseph Chapman and Guadalupe Ortega were among the latter group.

Meanwhile, political events were in motion that would ultimately mark the end to the mission system. Spain had once supported and encouraged the missions, but after Mexico declared its independence from Spain in 1821, the new government looked upon the missions with indifference, and made plans to dispose of this burden that they had inherited. Whereas Spain had officially looked upon the Indians as charges to be cared for, the Mexican government looked at them as they did the missions: a burden for which they wanted no responsibility.

Against this backdrop, the turning point in the relations between the Chumash and the missions at La Purísima Concepción and Santa Inés can be said to have occurred in 1824. Throughout Alta California and throughout the history of the missions, the affinity between the Indians and the missionaries was almost always better than that between the Indians and the civil authorities. Such was an incident that occurred at Santa Inés and escalated into a full-scale revolt the likes of which had not been seen in this relatively tranquil area.

At Mission Santa Inés on February 21, 1824, a military guard beat a Chumash neophyte from La Purísima Concepción. Though no missionary was involved, some of the Chumash rioted and set fire to portions of the quadrangle at Santa Inés, including the mission church. Other neophytes helped to put out the fire, while the rioters moved on to attack La Purísima Concepción. They seized Mission La Purísima Concepción and would hold it for about a month. When he heard of what had happened, the governor ordered a military response, and troops from the Presidio of Monterey were ordered to strike back. A three-hour battle at La Purísima Concepción left sixteen Chumash and one soldier dead. Father Rodríguez at La Purísima Concepción negotiated a surrender, but the authorities came down with a heavy hand. Seven of the leaders of the rebellion were executed and eighteen others were imprisoned.

Relations between the neophytes and the missionaries at the two missions returned to some degree of normalcy, but they would almost certainly never be as they had been before the rebellion. A decade later, the Secularization Act was ratified and the mission system collapsed. During his four-month term in early 1836, Governor Mariano Chico named José Covarrubias as the civilian administrator of Mission Santa Inés. He occupied a portion of mission property until about 1839.

In 1843, in an unusually charitable display, Governor Manuel Micheltorena cut a deal with Father Francisco Garcia Diego y Moreño, who was the first bishop of California, to transfer 35,499 acres of the now state-owned former Mission Santa Inés to the church for use as a Franciscan seminary. Known as the College of Our Lady of Refuge, it opened on the former mission grounds, but moved to another site a few miles to the east a year later.

After three years in office, Micheltorena was succeeded as governor of Alta California by the greedy Pío Pico. The last Mexican governor, Pico took office in 1845 on the eve of Alta California becoming part of the United States. He adopted a policy of selling off what was left of the former missions, which in most cases involved just the church and a few adjoining buildings. At Santa

Above: The Chapel of the Madonnas was installed during the extensive renovation work conducted at the mission by Father Alexander Buckler and his niece, Mamie Goulet, between 1904 and 1924. Beginning in 1992, paintings throughout the mission complex underwent restoration.

Opposite: In August 1989, the mission celebrated the completion of an extensive restoration project for the east wing. The major element of this project was the reconstruction of eight of the nineteen arches that form the eastern facade of the building, restoring the convento to nearly its original length.

Inés, there was now substantially more property, and in 1846 he sold this to the former administrator, José Covarrubias, and José Joaquin Carrillo for $7,000, the equivalent of about $140,000 today.

Despite the sale, both the College of Our Lady of Refuge and the Santa Inés mission church would continue to operate. The latter was administered by Father Francisco Sánchez and Father José Joaquin Jimeno as a satellite operation of the seminary until May 1850, when it was briefly taken over by the Picpus Fathers of the Sacred Hearts of Jesus and Mary. The following year, the United States government declared Pío Pico's seizure of Mission Santa Inés illegal, and Father Eugene O'Connell arrived to become the new pastor of the church. However, records show that it was not until May 23, 1862, that President Abraham Lincoln signed the paperwork formally returning Mission Santa Inés to the Catholic Church.

Because the original owners, the Franciscan Order, were not in residence at the mission, the title to the property went to the Diocese of Monterey. In turn, the diocese would sell off an estimated 20,000 acres of the mission lands, retaining approximately 16,000 acres.

The College of Our Lady of Refuge would continue to operate as a Franciscan seminary until 1877, when the administration of the school passed to the Christian Brothers. Four

years later, the seminary closed for budgetary reasons.

The church also suffered from a lack of funds. A number of structures were dangerously uninhabitable, and in 1884 a portion of the priests' quarters collapsed. However, an Irish family living on the property at this time worked to forestall a total deterioration of the buildings. The Donahues had arrived in 1882 and remained until 1898. During those years, they did a great deal of both routine and major work.

Also still living at Mission Santa Inés at this time were a number of aging former neophytes. One such man was Rafael Solares, a sacristan at the church who blended his adopted culture with his ancestral one by also being active as a Chumash shaman.

In July 1904, the Diocese of Monterey assigned Father Alexander Buckler as pastor of Mission Santa Inés and adjacent areas as far west as the Pacific Ocean. This included the city of Lompoc and the site of the old Mission La Purísima Concepción. Like Father John O'Sullivan at Mission San Juan Capistrano, Father Buckler was part of a new generation of priests who came to the California missions in the early twentieth century, fired with a vision of restoring the crumbling artifacts to their former glory.

One might say that they had a mission, and the missions were it. The energetic Father Buckler would serve at Santa Inés for two decades, taking it upon himself to stabilize and retrofit crumbling buildings and add badly needed new roofs. Aided by his niece, Mamie Goulet, he transformed the mission complex from a derelict to a campus that truly inspired pride. When the aging campanario collapsed in a winter storm in 1911, he had it rebuilt using reinforced concrete. He did take a bit of license in his design for this reconstruction by building the campanario with four, rather than the original three, niches for the bells. The mission bells were rehung in this new campanario in 1912.

Mamie Goulet is also credited with having done a great deal of important preservation work with the mission's collection of antique church vestments, which is the largest in California. The collection includes more than 500 garments dating back to the fifteenth century. The vestments include many that were used in Baja California, as well as those from Alta California. One of the latter was used by Father Serra himself.

Upon Father Buckler's retirement in November 1924, the Diocese of Monterey offered Mission Santa Inés to the Capuchin Franciscan Order of the Irish Province. They would continue the restoration, bringing the mission into the twentieth century with electrical service and indoor plumbing.

After World War II, the Capuchins concentrated on restoration work that would make Mission Santa Inés better resemble its pre-1812 configuration. The campanario

that Father Buckler had dedicated in 1912 was modified to its nineteenth-century appearance with three bell niches. This project was largely complete by the time that the mission celebrated its 150th anniversary in 1954. In this year, a statue of Our Lady of Lourdes was brought in from Oberammergau in Germany to be placed near the cemetery, and one of the older mission bells was recast in Rotterdam.

Earthquake retrofit work would take place during the 1970s, and restoration of the convento wing of the mission to its early nineteenth-century appearance would take place in the 1980s. The completion of the latter project was formally celebrated at the eighteenth annual Mission Santa Inés Fiesta in August 1989. The wing that had once housed the Franciscan missionaries now housed a parish hall and conference center. In the meantime, two new bells, called "Saint Francis" and, of course, "Santa Inés," were cast and hung in the campanario in 1984.

Beginning in the 1990s, restoration work turned to the paintings inside the mission church. Other work involved restoration of the Chumash village, the addition of a Chumash memorial, and a complete archaeological excavation of the quadrangle and adjacent buildings. In September 2004, Mission Santa Inés celebrated its bicentennial with an anniversary weekend program that included wine tasting, jazz, and historic reenactments.

CHAPTER TWENTY

MISSION SAN RAFAEL ARCÁNGEL

FOLLOWING THE DEDICATION OF Mission Santa Inés in 1804, no new missions would be added to the Alta California mission system for thirteen or seventeen years. This discrepancy is derived from the question of when one fixes the establishment of the twentieth mission. Mission San Rafael Arcángel was founded in 1817, but as an asistencia, or satellite mission, of Mission San Francisco de Asís, which was across the Golden Gate to the south. San Rafael Arcángel would not be upgraded to full mission status until 1823, after Alta California was transferred from Spain to Mexico. As such, it was the only asistencia in the mission system to become a mission.

The establishment of an asistencia on the north side of the Golden Gate in what is now California's Marin County was the subject of discussions as early as 1816 between Governor Pablo Vicente de Solá and Father Ramón Abella at Mission San Francisco de Asís. Father Abella recommended that such a facility could

be used by sick neophytes who were adversely impacted by the heavy fog and bitterly cold weather that is experienced annually during the early summer in the area surrounding his mission. Lieutenant Gabriel Moraga, based at the Presidio of San Francisco, recommended a site near an inlet about a dozen miles north of the Golden Gate that he had previously surveyed. The site, known to the native Ohlone people as Awaniwi or Nanaguami, was approved in 1817, and Alta California mission system Father-Prefect (later Father-President) Vicente Francisco Sarría came north for the dedication.

On December 13, Father Sarría crossed the Golden Gate in the company of a group of Spanish soldiers, including Lieutenant Luis Argüello, the commandant of the Presidio of San Francisco, and several Franciscans, including Father Luis Gil y Taboada, who would serve for two years as the first senior missionary at the new asistencia. San Rafael Arcángel was formally dedicated by Father Sarría with a cel-

Above: An artist's conception of Mission San Rafael as it originally appeared.
Opposite: A wide-angle view of the mission courtyard as it appears today, with St. Raphael Church on the left and the 1949 mission church replica on the right.

ebratory Mass on December 14, 1817. It was named for St. Raphael, a patron of healing, and one of three archangels that are mentioned in the Bible. The other two, Gabriel and Michael, had previously been namesakes for other Alta California missions.

In 1818, several adobe buildings were built, including the church and a large structure forty-two feet wide and

eighty-seven feet long that housed living quarters and a hospital for the ailing neophytes that were brought across from Mission San Francisco de Asís. As befitted the status of San Rafael Arcángel as an asistencia, the church was a simple one, without a campanario, and there was no effort made to build a complete quadrangle. Despite the modest size of the new

complex, it is recorded to have had nearly 400 residents by the end of its first year.

In 1819, Father Gil was succeeded by Father Juan Amoros, who came north from Mission San Carlos Borromeo de Carmelo in Carmel. Two years later, Mexico declared its independence from Spain and the political landscape in Alta California abruptly changed. In general, the Mexican government saw little to be gained from a continued support of the mission system. This official indifference would lead ultimately to the liquidation of the missions through the ratification of the Secularization Act in 1834. However, in the case of the missions in the north, the Mexicans could see some immediate political value.

A half-century earlier, the Spanish government had actively promoted the notion of missions north of Monterey for political reasons. By founding missions—as well as settlements and a presidio—around the San Francisco Bay Area, Spain established a physical presence in territory that it had claimed but not previously occupied. In 1822, as Mexico digested its recent acquisition of Alta California, the Russians were expanding their presence on the coast of California, and there was a major Russian post just fifty miles north of San Rafael Arcángel—closer to the mission than Monterey.

The Russian fur hunters had been probing the western coast of North America, specifically what is now southern Alaska, since about 1742. They had

Above: This watercolor image by Henry Chapman Ford shows the mission church with just a single star-shaped window above the door. A highly regarded painter of California scenes, Chapman lived in Santa Barbara from 1875 until his death in 1894. He would have visited San Rafael after the original mission was torn down.

Opposite: The 1949 replica church had a bell frame similar to that which appears in the Chapman watercolor.

Contact Information:
MISSION SAN RAFAEL ARCÁNGEL
1104 Fifth Avenue
San Rafael, CA 94901
Phone: (415) 454-8141

Web site:
www.saintraphael.com

established a permanent settlement on Kodiak Island in 1784, at a time when nine of the twenty-one Franciscan missions existed in Alta California. The city of New Archangel, now Sitka, was established in what is now the Alaska panhandle in 1799, the year after Father Fermín Lasuén founded Mission San Luis Rey de Francia. Early in the nineteenth century, Alexander Baranov of the Russian-American Company began searching for furs farther south. In 1804, he sent Ivan Alexandrovich Kuskov to survey sites north of San Francisco Bay for a possible Russian outpost. This was desirable because the climate was better than in Alaska, and because the potential for furs had not yet been tapped. Kuskov spent eight months exploring the coast that Sir Francis Drake had

called New Albion. He then returned north with 2,000 sea otter pelts and several site recommendations.

Early in 1812, Kuskov returned to New Albion with the ship *Chirikov*, and went ashore north of Bodega Bay at a place referred to by the local Kashaya Pomo people as Meteni. In August 1812, five years before the Spanish established the asistencia at San Rafael Arcángel, the Russian-American Company dedicated the fort that would come to be known as Fort Ross, a shortened form of Rossiya, or Russia.

A Russian-American Company ship had sailed into San Francisco Bay in April 1806, marking the first significant contact between the Spanish and the Russians in Alta California. The Spanish could imagine this as the first

step in what had the potential to become a major confrontation. While the presence of the Russians was of concern to the Spanish, it was more so to the Mexicans. This thought was certainly in the mind of the Mexican authorities when Asistencia San Rafael Arcángel was rededicated as Mission San Rafael Arcángel on October 19, 1822. By that time, plans were already in motion for the establishment of a second mission, San Francisco Solano, north of the Golden Gate.

Under Father Amoros, Mission San Rafael Arcángel would expand and flourish. Its total agricultural output would exceed that of many other Northern California missions, including San Francisco de Asís, Santa Cruz, and San Juan Bautista—even though they had been in operation for much longer.

Through 1832, San Rafael Arcángel would produce 3,730 tons of crops, including its famous pears, and 2,087 tons of wheat, the staple crop at each of the missions. In terms of the annual average, San Rafael Arcángel was second only to Mission San José's 318 tons, with 249 tons of all crops combined. This is compared to 104 tons at San Carlos Borromeo de Carmelo, ninety-nine tons at both San Juan Bautista and Santa Clara de Asís, and just sixty-seven tons at San Francisco de Asís. For wheat production, San Rafael Arcángel actually had the largest annual average in Northern California with 139 tons, compared to 108 tons at Mission San José.

Above: Like the mission church, St. Raphael Church features a shaped window over the doorway. Opposite: Warm sunlight bathes the peaceful interior of the Mission San Rafael replica church.

On the spiritual side, there were 1,821 people baptized at San Rafael Arcángel through the end of 1832, beginning with the twenty-six baptisms that had occurred on the first day in 1817. During those fifteen years, 519 weddings would be performed. These were among the fewest performed at any of the missions, but this detail should be evaluated against the fact that San Rafael Arcángel was a mission for just ten of those fifteen years.

Father Amoros passed away at Mission San Rafael Arcángel in 1832, on the eve of secularization. He was replaced by the reckless Father José María Mercado of the Zacatecan Franciscans. In a single incident, the new priest would undo essentially all of the goodwill that Father Gil and Father Amoros had built up during all their years at San Rafael Arcángel. His abrasive manner earned him few friends among the Ohlone and Coast Miwok neophyte population, but the straw that broke the camel's back came when Father Mercado armed a group of neophytes to ambush a group of Pomo people that he mistakenly thought were going to attack the mission. The ensuing firefight resulted in the deaths of more than twenty unarmed Pomo. Both the native and Spanish population in the San Francisco Bay Area were outraged at this incident, and Father Mercado was relieved of his pastorship and disciplined.

In 1834, the Secularization Act was ratified, and General Mariano Vallejo, the commandant at the Presidio of San Francisco, was named as civilian administrator of both Mission San Rafael Arcángel and Mission San Francisco Solano. He quickly moved to carry out the process of relieving the mission of its property. Much of the mission lands associated with both missions would find their way into Vallejo's own real estate portfolio, and many neophytes found themselves working for room and board on Vallejo's ranchos.

The Russians at Fort Ross, meanwhile, would remain until 1841. When they departed, they sold the property to John Sutter, the Swiss-born Californian who was a staunch advocate of incorporating Alta California into the United States. It was on another Sutter property across the state, near Coloma, that James Marshall would make the legendary discovery in 1848 that initiated the California gold rush.

In July 1846, the Bear Flag Revolt—which occurred across the street from Mission San Francisco Solano in the city of Sonoma—touched off the rapidly moving series of events that would result in California becoming part of the United States.

As the U.S. Navy landed in Monterey, U.S. Army forces under Colonel John C. Frémont moved through California to solidify American control. During this time, Colonel Frémont would briefly make use of the buildings at Mission San Rafael Arcángel.

The following year, a priest was assigned to the mission church at San Rafael Arcángel. This church, which had originally been built as a simple asistencia chapel, suffered from deferred maintenance and gradual collapse, even as the growing city of San Rafael was gradually taking shape around it. The United States returned six and a half acres of land to the church in 1855, but by then the building was in ruins. A new church was built next to these ruins in 1861, and a larger church was constructed on the original site in 1870 to serve as the centerpiece of St. Raphael Parish. As the story goes, by that time the only thing left of the original Mission San Rafael Arcángel was a single pear tree.

In 1949, under the direction of Monsignor Thomas Kennedy, a chapel was constructed a short distance down the hill from St. Raphael Church, at approximately the place where the hospital had been built 131 years earlier. Based on nineteenth-century paintings and engravings that exist, this church was built to be as close a replica as possible to the original mission church, although the convento that was attached to the right side of the old mission church was not constructed.

St. Raphael Church and the mission replica are today located at the center of the city of San Rafael, the county seat and largest city in Marin County. The parish also includes St. Raphael Parochial School, an elementary school serving kindergarten through eighth grade. Founded in 1889, it is operated by the Dominican Sisters of San Rafael. Dating back to 1890, the Dominican University of California is also located in the city of San Rafael, across town from the old mission site.

CHAPTER TWENTY-ONE

MISSION SAN FRANCISCO SOLANO

Nearly two decades would elapse between the dedication of the nineteen missions south of the Golden Gate and the two northern missions. The first, Mission San Rafael Arcángel, involved upgrading an asistencia, or satellite mission, founded in 1817, and the second was Mission San Francisco Solano, the last mission to be founded in the Alta California chain.

With the establishment of Mission Santa Inés in 1804, the chain of missions had been considered complete. There were no gaps left to fill between Mission San Diego de Alcalá and Mission San Francisco de Asís, and no plans to establish any missions north of the Golden Gate.

During his two years as the first senior missionary at Asistencia San Rafael Arcángel, Father Luis Gil y Taboada traveled north to the upper reaches of San Francisco Bay and east into the Sacramento River delta as far as present-day Suisun City, and recommended new mission sites, but no steps would be taken to act upon these recommendations. The mission system was considered complete.

By 1822, as possession of Alta California had passed from Spain to Mexico, plans were underway to upgrade San Rafael Arcángel from asistencia to mission status. However, there would not have been another, all-new mission north of the Golden Gate had it not been for Father José Altimira. Recalled as an ambitious and abrasive fellow, he had arrived in Alta California from Spain just three years earlier, and he had been posted to Mission San Francisco de Asís. While there, he hatched a grand plan under which San Francisco de Asís would be closed at its present location and moved to a site north of San Francisco Bay and twenty-one miles north of Mission San Rafael Arcángel.

Known to the native people of the region as Sonoma, it is the site of the present-day California city of the same name. Father Altimira, of course, saw himself as the senior missionary at this new mission. His plan even called for San Rafael Arcángel to

Above: The mission church as it appeared in about 1925. The bell has not yet been hung. Opposite: The simple altar in the mission church is backed by a painted reredos.

remain as an asistencia controlled by this new mission.

Instead of presenting his scheme to Father-President José Francisco de Paula Señan, Father Altimira took it to Mexican Governor Luis Argüello in 1823. While the Mexican government had little interest in perpetuating the mission system, Argüello did recognize the political value of having another outpost north of San Francisco Bay. The Russians were just fifty miles away at Fort Ross, and there were Americans settling nearly everywhere

Above: The steeple added in the 1850s was not removed until the mission church was restored following the 1906 earthquake.

throughout the northern part of Alta California. Though it was not technically within his power to do so, Governor Argüello approved Father Altimira's plan, which was endorsed by the Alta California legislature in Monterey, which also was without the power to authorize a new mission. This power lay with Father-President Señan, who was, unfortunately, then lying on his deathbed at Mission San Buenaventura.

Father-President Señan briefed his successor, Father Vicente Francisco de Sarría, on the situation, and Father Sarría intervened immediately. He contacted Governor Argüello, and a compromise was

worked out whereby the new mission at Sonoma would be established, but Mission San Francisco de Asís would stay and Mission San Rafael Arcángel would be independent of either mission.

On July 4, 1823, Father Altimira formally dedicated the new mission as Mission San Francisco Solano. It would be named for St. Francis Solano, or Solanus, a Spanish-born Franciscan missionary who worked with the native peoples of what are now Paraguay and Peru during the seventeenth century. Born in Cordova in Spain on March 10, 1549, he joined the Franciscan Order at Montilla at age twenty and was sent to South

America in 1589. A gifted linguist, he is said to have mastered many indigenous languages throughout the areas where he worked. He also is recalled for having an ability to predict the future. He is said to have predicted earthquakes and his own death. His final post was as guardian of the Franciscan convent in Lima, Peru, where he passed away on July 14, 1610. Father Solano was beatified by Pope Clement X in 1675, and canonized by Pope Benedict XIII in 1726.

Father Altimira, who had begun work on the buildings for his new mission when he still thought it was going to be a relocated Mission San Francisco de Asís, went back to work,

and a wood-frame church was ready for dedication in 1824. Ironically, many of the ecclesiastical supplies that were used at the church would be donated by Mission San Francisco de Asís. In another turn of irony, the mission bells were donated by the Russians.

One of Father Altimira's selling points for his plan to move Mission San Francisco de Asís had been his promise that agricultural production would be greater at the Sonoma location. As it turned out, he was wrong. The annual average agricultural production would be the least of any of the missions, less even than San Francisco de Asís. A total of just 549 tons of crops would be produced on the mission lands. The annual average was sixty-one tons, compared to sixty-seven tons at Mission San Francisco de Asís. On the other hand, San Francisco Solano can be credited with laying the foundation for what would be, by far, the region's most important crop in the ensuing two centuries. By 1825, the missionaries had planted the first vineyard in the Sonoma Valley, which today ranks second only to the neighboring Napa Valley among the premier wine-growing appellations in the United States.

Through the end of 1832, a total of 1,008 baptisms and 263 weddings would be performed at the mission. As might be expected for the mission established last, these figures were the lowest of any of the missions in the Alta California chain. Due perhaps to the conceited temperament of Father

Above: A group of neophytes gather at Sonoma, circa 1827, for what appears to be a traditional celebration. Some are dressed in European clothing, but the man who is the center of attention wears traditional garb. Note the dome-shaped neophyte homes at the right.

Contact Information:
MISSION SAN FRANCISCO SOLANO
114 East Spain Street
Sonoma, CA 95476
Phone: (707) 938-1519

Sonoma State Historic Park
363 Third Street West
Sonoma, California 95476
Phone: (707) 938-9560

California State Parks Web site:
www.parks.ca.gov

Altimira, relations between the native people and Mission San Francisco Solano were generally strained.

The native people living near Mission San Francisco Solano were different ethnically than those generally encountered at the missions south of San Francisco Bay. Located north of the traditional homeland of the Ohlone people of the San Francisco Bay Area, Sonoma was a place frequented by several distinct peoples. Two of these spoke dialects of a linguistic group that anthropologists refer to as Penutian, one spoke a Yukian language, and another, the Pomo, spoke a separate, Pomoan language. The Pomo were one of the most numerous tribes in northern California. Their traditional lands extended from the Pacific Ocean inland to the mountains east of Clear Lake and far into the northern part of the state. The Yukian speakers in the area, who are best known as Wappo, lived in and around the valleys of the Russian River and the Napa River north of Mission San Francisco Solano.

To the west were the Coast Miwok, a people who also interacted with the missionaries at Mission San Rafael Arcángel. They were one branch of a family of peoples that included the Lake Miwok, who lived to the north in the area of Clear Lake, and the main Miwok group, who lived on the western slope of the Sierra Nevada between the Fresno and Cosumnes rivers, notably including Yosemite Valley. To the north and east were the Penutian-speaking Wintun people, whose traditional homeland was the western side of the Sacramento Valley as far north as the Trinity River.

Though the three tribes were linguistically distinct from the tribes south of San Francisco Bay, they were culturally similar to the southern inland tribes. Like many of these peoples, they were hunter-gatherers, whose gathering centered primarily on the acorns from the abundant oak trees that covered the hills and filled the river valleys. These they ground into paste for baking. The wildlife they hunted would have been mainly deer and smaller animals, although elk and bear were also present in the area.

Father Altimira may have gotten along well with the Mexican government officials, but his irritating manner annoyed the potential neophytes and eventually led to disaster. Two of the worst incidents involving overt Indian hostility toward the missions involved Mission San Diego de Alcalá, the first and most southern in the chain, and Mission San Francisco Solano, the last and most northern. In 1775, the former was attacked and burned to the ground. Just over a half-century later, in 1826, the same fate befell Mission San Francisco Solano.

The attack, which destroyed the church and other buildings, is directly linked to Father Altimira's harsh treatment of neophytes, which included beatings and floggings. Finally, the Indians reached a point where they felt they'd had enough.

So too, apparently, had Father-President Narciso Durán. Father Altimira had escaped to Mission San Rafael Arcángel during the attack, but he would not return. Instead of reassigning Father Altimira to rebuild Mission San Francisco Solano, Father-President Durán assigned the task to Father Buenaventura Fortuni, who had been his assistant when he was the senior missionary at Mission San José. Father Altimira's reputation had rendered him no longer welcome in Alta California, and he was sent back to Spain.

Father Fortuni's reconstruction efforts centered not only on replacing the church and other buildings, but the reputation of the mission. By 1832, there were thirty structures in the mission complex, including the new church and a twenty-seven-room convento. In that same year, Father Fortuni's sixth at the mission, he was able to post the best record in its short history, both in terms of agricultural production and in relations with the neophyte population. There were now 996 neophytes in residence at Mission San Francisco Solano, and the 127 baptisms and thirty-four weddings conducted that year were the most yet recorded. Unfortunately, it was not to last.

During the following spring, a storm did considerable damage to the rebuilt church, and by the end of the year, the Secularization Act was awaiting ratification. Father Fortuni retired in 1833 after nearly seven years, turning Mission San Francisco Solano over

to Father José Gutiérrez, a Mexican-born Zacatecan Franciscan priest. The mission church at San Francisco Solano became a parish church on November 3, 1834, and Father Gutiérrez was later succeeded by Father José Lorenzo Quijas.

With secularization, General Mariano Vallejo, the commandant at the Presidio of San Francisco, became the civilian administrator for both Mission San Rafael Arcángel and Mission San Francisco Solano. He quickly added the mission lands to his own property, and the neophytes found themselves at work in fields that were now under his ownership.

The following year, General Vallejo moved to the area himself and officially established the Sonoma Pueblo, which would evolve into today's city of Sonoma. This settlement quickly grew up around the former mission, even as the old mission complex deteriorated. Bricks and roof tiles from the collapsed buildings were used in constructing new buildings that started to ring the broad plaza at the center of the new city. Vallejo's own home was a large adobe structure that faced the north side of the plaza. It was directly across what is now First Street East from Mission San Francisco Solano. By 1841, the church itself was in such bad condition that Vallejo himself ordered it torn down and replaced by a new adobe church on the same site.

In 1845, Governor Pío Pico seized all of the remaining mission

churches in Alta California and began selling them to private parties, notably his friends and business associates. There were no takers for the one at San Francisco Solano, so it remained essentially unchanged. The following year, however, big changes would sweep Alta California, and Sonoma would be the unlikely epicenter.

By the summer of 1846, the winds of war that would result in California becoming part of the United States were beginning to blow at gale force. Before that, however, California would be briefly declared as an independent republic, and that declaration would be made at Sonoma.

In March, a U.S. Army force under Colonel John C. Frémont had been involved in a brief standoff with former Mexican Governor José María Castro at Gavilan Peak, near Mission San Juan Bautista, and Frémont would remain in Alta California on a scouting expedition. In April, Mexican General Mariano Arista invaded Texas, and on May 13 the United States declared war on Mexico, marking the beginning of the Mexican War.

At the break of dawn on June 14, California became a republic. In what would be known as the Bear Flag Revolt, a group of American settlers surrounded General Vallejo's fortified home on the plaza, demanding that he surrender. Vallejo put on his dress uniform and invited the group to send in three representatives. Over breakfast and a few glasses of wine, he explained that he had been looking

forward to California becoming part of the United States, and he would be happy to surrender.

The next step in the Bear Flag Revolt would be the raising of that flag and the declaration of the republic. The flag itself was designed by William Todd, a nephew of Mary Todd Lincoln, the wife of Illinois congressional candidate Abraham Lincoln, who would be elected as the sixteenth president of the United States in 1860. The flag consisted of a tan piece of cloth with a red strip sewn to the bottom. On this, Todd lettered the words "California Republic" and drew a red star—to symbolize solidarity with the recently invaded Texas—as well as a California golden bear, cousin to the grizzly of the Rockies, the most powerful animal indigenous to California. Thus created, the Bear Flag was run up the flagpole in the plaza in Sonoma, and California was briefly a republic.

Unlike the Republic of Texas, which had remained independent for a decade before joining the United States in 1845, the Republic of California would last just a few weeks. It ceased to exist before the news that it had been a republic had reached many corners of the state. The U.S. Navy, under Commodore John Sloat, captured the Mexican provincial capital at Monterey on July 7, and two days later the United States flag went up in the village of Yerba Buena, which would soon become the city of San Francisco. Replaced by the stars and stripes, the Bear Flag of the California Republic was later adapted as the model for the official flag of the state of California. The design was fine-tuned several times, with the present flag having been finalized in 1953.

Jailed briefly after his arrest in 1846, Mariano Vallejo returned to Sonoma. In 1849, he served as a delegate to the state constitutional convention, and after California achieved statehood, he served as a state senator.

The church at the former Mission San Francisco Solano continued to serve off and on as a parish church, but it suffered greatly from deferred maintenance. By 1881, it had deteriorated to the point where it was considered not worth upgrading. The archbishop of San Francisco, Joseph Sadoc Alemany, decided to dispose of the property and use the proceeds to defray the cost of building a new church elsewhere in Sonoma. Originally sold to a man named Solomon Shocken, the buildings in the mission complex would serve a variety of purposes through the coming years. The church became a warehouse, the priests' living quarters were used as a blacksmith shop, other structures served as barns, and the convento is said to have once been a winery.

The former vineyards at Mission San Francisco Solano went through a series of owners until 1904, when they were sold to an immigrant from the Tuscany region of Italy named Samuele Sebastiani. The Sebastiani family vineyards and winery would

flourish through the years, and today, this family-owned company is one of the Sonoma Valley's leading vintners. The Sebastiani name is widely recognized around the world.

As for the mission itself, it was acquired in 1903 by the California Historic Landmarks League, the organization that was leading the restoration work at Mission San Carlos Borromeo de Carmelo and at Mission San Antonio de Padua with funding from newspaper publisher William Randolph Hearst. A great deal of work had been done toward the restoration of the church by the morning of April 18, 1906, when the ground began to shake violently. It is called the Great San Francisco Earthquake because that city was the largest population center affected, but the epicenter was actually nearer to Sonoma. Every mission from San Juan Bautista north was affected by the earthquake, some more than others. Ironically, Mission San Francisco de Asís in San Francisco suffered minor harm, while Mission San Francisco Solano was badly damaged. The Landmarks League picked up the pieces and continued their work. By 1913, the mission had been restored and opened as a museum of Sonoma history.

The California Historic Landmarks League donated the property in 1926 to the California Division of Beaches and Parks, the predecessor to today's Department of Parks and Recreation. During the mid-1940s, the

Above: A coat of stucco applied in 1944 returned the church to its original appearance.

State of California resumed work at the mission church to fully restore it to the way that it appeared, inside and out, during the mission period. The convento was also remodeled with an eye toward historic authenticity. Along

with General Vallejo's fortified residence overlooking the plaza, and other structures, Mission San Francisco Solano became part of the Sonoma State Historic Park, and it remains as such today.

Appendixes

I. Franciscan Missions in Alta California (Now the State of California)

Mission San Diego de Alcalá (1769)
Mission San Carlos Borromeo de Carmelo (1770)
Mission San Antonio de Padua (1771)
Mission San Gabriel Arcángel (1771)
Mission San Luis Obispo de Tolosa (1772)
Mission San Francisco de Asís (1776)
Mission San Juan Capistrano (1776)
Mission Santa Clara de Asís (1777)
Mission San Buenaventura (1782)
Mission Santa Bárbara (1786)
Mission La Purísima Concepción (1787)
Mission Santa Cruz (1791)
Mission Nuestra Señora de la Soledad (1791)
Mission San José de Guadalupe (1797)
Mission San Juan Bautista (1797)
Mission San Miguel Arcángel (1797)
Mission San Fernando Rey de España (1797)
Mission San Luis Rey de Francia (1798)
Mission Santa Inés (1804)
Mission San Rafael Arcángel (1817)
Mission San Francisco de Solano (1823)

II. Jesuit Missions in Baja California and Baja California Sur

Misión San Bruno (1683–1685)
Misión Nuestra Señora de Loreto Conchó (1697–1829)
Visita de San Juan Bautista Londó (1699–1745)
Misión San Francisco Javier Vigge Biaundó (1699–1817)
Misión San Juan Bautista Malbat (1705–1721)
Misión Santa Rosalia de Mulegé (1705–1828)
Misión San Jose de Comondú (1708–1827)
Misión La Purísima Concepción de Cadegomó (1720–1822)
Misión de Nuestra Señora del Pilar de La Paz Airapí (1720–1749)
Misión Nuestra Señora de Guadalupe de Huasinapi (1720–1795)
Misión Santiago de Los Coras (1721–1795)
Misión Nuestra Señora de los Dolores del Sur Chillá (1721–1768)
Misión San Ignacio Kadakaamán (1728–1840)
Misión Estero de las Palmas de San José del Cabo Añuití (1730–1840)
Misión Santa Rosa de las Palmas (Todos Santos) (1733–1840)
Misión San Luis Gonzaga Chiriyaqui (1740–1768)
Misión Santa Gertrudis (1752–1822)
Misión San Francisco Borja (1762–1818)
Visita de Calamajué (1766–1767)
Misión Santa María de los Angeles (1767–1768)
Franciscan Establishments (1768–1773)
Misión San Fernando Rey de España de Velicatá (1769–1818)
Visita de la Presentación (1769–1817)

III. Dominican Missions in Baja California and Baja California Sur

Misión Nuestra Señora del Santísimo Rosario de Viñacado (1774–1832)
Visita de San José de Magdalena (1774–1828)
Misión Santo Domingo de la Frontera (1775–1839)
Misión San Vicente Ferrer (1780–1833)
Misión San Miguel Arcángel de la Frontera (1797–1834)
Misión Santo Tomás de Aquino (1791–1849)
Misión San Pedro Mártir de Verona (1794–1824)
Misión Santa Catalina Vírgen y Mártir (1797–1840)
Visita de San Telmo (1798–1839)
Misión El Descanso (San Miguel la Nueva) (1817–1834)
Misión Nuestra Señora de Guadalupe del Norte (1834–1840)

IV. Father-Presidents of the Alta California Mission System

1769–1784 Father Junípero Serra
1784–1785 Father Francisco Palóu (acting)
1785–1803 Father Fermín Francisco de Lasuén
1803–1812 Father Pedro Estévan Tápis
1812–1815 Father José Francisco de Paula Señan
1815–1819 Father Mariano Payeras
1820–1823 Father José Francisco de Paula Señan
1823–1824 Father Vicente Francisco de Sarría
1824–1827 Father Narciso Durán
1827–1830 Father José Bernardo Sánchez
1830–1838 Father Narciso Durán
1838–1844 Father José Joaquin Jimeno
1844–1846 Father Narciso Durán

V. Headquarters of the Alta California Mission System:

1769–1771: Mission San Diego de Alcalá
1771–1815: Mission San Carlos Borromeo de Carmelo
1815–1819: Mission La Purísima Concepción*
1819–1824: Mission San Carlos Borromeo de Carmelo
1824–1827: Mission San José*
1827–1830: Mission San Carlos Borromeo de Carmelo
1830–1833: Mission San José*
1833–1846: Mission Santa Bárbara

* While Father Payeras and Father Durán (until 1833) served as father-president, they remained at the missions where they had been in residence, so these missions became the de facto headquarters during their terms.

GLOSSARY OF TERMS

VI. GOVERNORS OF ALTA CALIFORNIA DURING THE MISSION PERIOD

Spanish Governors:
1768–1770: Don Gaspar de Portolá
1770–1774: Felipe de Barri (political)
1770–1774: Pedro Fages (military)
1774–1777: Fernando Rivera y Moncada
1777–1782: Felipe de Neve
1782–1791: Pedro Fages
1791–1792: José Antonio Romeu
1792–1794: José Joaquin de Arrillaga
1794–1800: Diego de Borica
1800: Pedro de Alberni (acting)
1800–1814: José Joaquin de Arrillaga
1814–1815: José Dario Argüello
1815–1822: Pablo Vicente de Solá

Mexican Governors:
1822: Pablo Vicente de Solá
1822–1825: Luis Antonio Argüello
1825–1831: José María de Echeandía
1831: Manuel Victoria
1831–1832: Pío de Jesus Pico
1832–1833: Augustin V. Zamorano
    (northern Alta California)
1832–1833: José María de Echeandía
    (southern Alta California)
1833–1835: José Figueroa
1835: José Castro
1835–1836: Nicolas Gutiérrez
1836: Mariano Chico
1836: Nicolas Gutiérrez
1836–1842: Juan Bautista Alvarado
1836: José Castro (contra government)
1842–1845: Manuel Micheltorena
1845–1846: Pío de Jesus Pico

VII: VICEROYS OF NEW SPAIN DURING THE MISSION PERIOD

1766–1771: Carlos Francisco de Croix, Marques de Croix
1771–1779: Antonio María de Bucareli y Ursua
1779–1783: Martin de Mayorga
1783–1784: Matias de Gálvez
1785–1786: Bernardo de Gálvez, Conde de Gálvez
1787: Alonso Nuñez de Haro y Peralta
1787–1789: Manuel Antonio Flores
1789–1794: Juan Vicente de Guemes Pacheco y Padilla, Conde de Revilla Gigedo II
1794–1798: Miguel de la Grua Talamanca y Branciforte, Marques de Branciforte
1798–1800: Miguel José de Azanza
1800–1803: Felix Berenguer de Marquina
1803–1808: José de Iturrigaray
1808–1809: Pedro Garibay
1809–1810: Francisco Javier de Lizana y Beaumont
1810–1813: Francisco Javier de Venegas
1813–1816: Felix María Calleja del Rey
1816–1821: Juan Ruiz de Apodaca, Conde del Venadito
1821: Francisco Novella
1821: Juan de O'Donojú (appointed without taking office)

This glossary is designed to serve as a reference to some of the terminology that is used in this book, and to terms which the reader may encounter elsewhere in studying the missions and the mission era.

ADOBE: Bricks made of compressed mud and straw that are dried in the sun.

ALCALDE: The mayor or justice of the peace of a town or a pueblo.

ASISTENCIA: A satellite mission.

BUTTRESS: A structure made of stone or wood that is built against a wall to strengthen it.

CAMPANARIO: A bell tower, or a wall that holds bells.

CLOISTER: An enclosed area that is separated from the rest of the mission complex.

CONVENTO: A building adjacent to a mission church where priests lived and worked. It was usually attached to the church.

LAVANDERÍA: The mission laundry, it was usually located outside the quadrangle.

MONJERÍO: A dormitory for young, unmarried women and widows.

NAVE: The main part of the church between the altar and main entrance where the congregation sits, stands, or kneels during services.

NEOPHYTE: A baptized Indian who had converted to Christianity, and who lived and worked at the mission.

PRESIDIO: A military post. There were four in Alta California, at San Francisco, Monterey, Santa Bárbara, and San Diego. They were established by the Spanish and became Mexican in 1822. They were occupied by the U.S. Army after 1846.

PUEBLO: A town or settlement.

QUADRANGLE: An enclosed courtyard or patio, with buildings on four sides.

RANCHERÍA: A Spanish term for an Indian camp or settlement.

REREDOS: A decorated wall structure located behind the main altar in a mission church.

SACRISTY: From the Latin *sacrastia*, a vestry or room in a church where the vestments, church furnishings, sacred vessels, and other treasures are kept, and where the priests prepare for ecclesiastical functions.

SANCTUARY: The area inside a church where the main altar is found.

SECULARIZATION: The process of changing something from religious to nonreligious, such as government confiscation of church property. The process of secularizing the Alta California missions began in 1834.

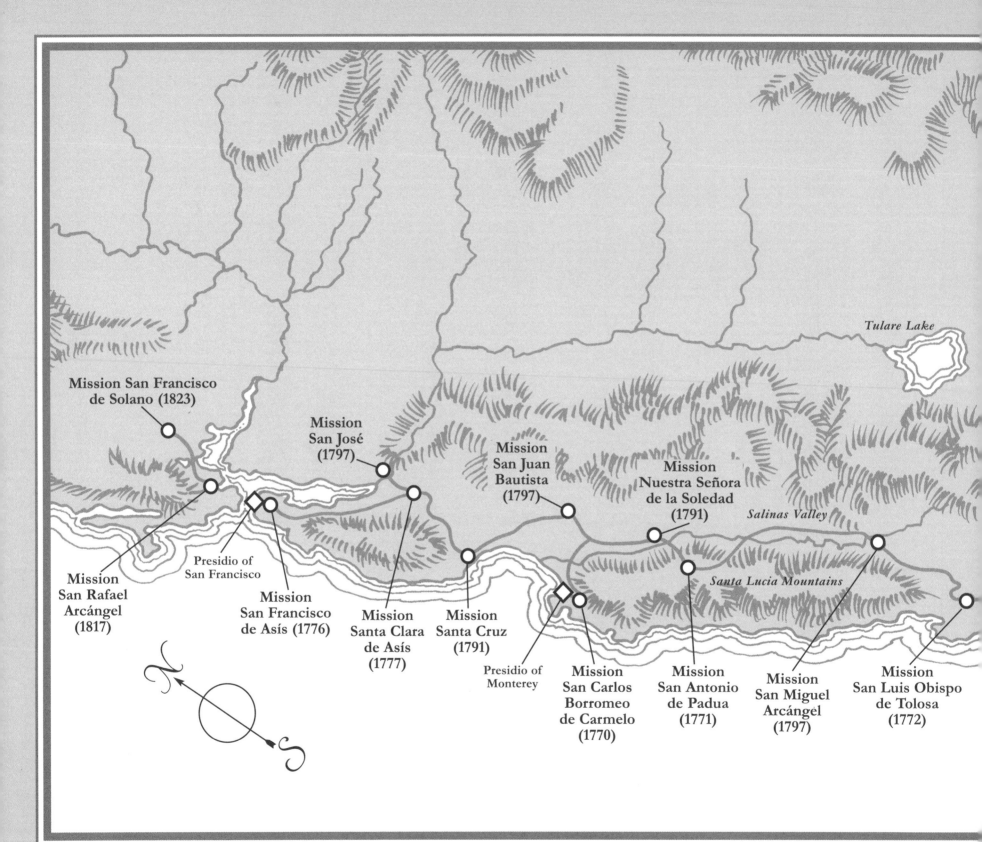

Mission San Francisco
de Solano (1823)

Mission
San José
(1797)

Mission
San Juan
Bautista
(1797)

Mission
Nuestra Señora
de la Soledad
(1791)

Tulare Lake

Salinas Valley

Presidio of
San Francisco

Mission
San Rafael
Arcángel
(1817)

Mission
San Francisco
de Asís (1776)

Mission
Santa Clara
de Asís
(1777)

Mission
Santa Cruz
(1791)

Santa Lucia Mountains

Presidio of
Monterey

Mission
San Carlos
Borromeo
de Carmelo
(1770)

Mission
San Antonio
de Padua
(1771)

Mission
San Miguel
Arcángel
(1797)

Mission
San Luis Obispo
de Tolosa
(1772)

N

S